a Bird's eye view of the Bible

by

Noah Quarshie

Copyright © 1983
Outreach - Ministries
N. Abington Rd.
Clarks Green, Penna.
Library of Congress Catalog Card Number: 83-61523
ISBN 0-9611544-0-3

Printed in United States of America

___ PREFACE ___

Today there are many editions of the Bible. Some editors claim they want to produce a simplified version of the Bible for the average reader.

However, during my undergraduate and graduate studies, I felt a strong need, not for a *simplified* Bible, but for a Bible study guide that would fulfill a need among laymen and new Christians that other books on Bible study were not meeting. I found many study books by Biblical writers are either oversimplified or directed towards the college student and are beyond the ability of the layman to use effectively.

This synoptic survey approaches the Bible as God's inspired, authoritative revelation without omission and without error. It is a spiritual guidebook to instruct and direct the believer for meaningful Godly living. The purpose of God set forth by each writer of the Bible and theme of each book is clearly outlined so that the layman and the new believer may prayerfully study the Bible by the help of the Holy Spirit with understanding and joy.

I wish to express my thanks to those who have contributed their time and effort in seeing the completion of this book: first to Mrs Ethel King, Baptist Bible School of Theology, who typed the final draft; special thanks to Mrs Edward (Esther) Oliver of Shelton College English Department who offered very valuable suggestions concerning mechanics and style; the help and suggestions of many faculty members and friends of Shelton College; and finally a deep appreciation to Miss Ruth Trato for her unique role in the publication of the book.

Dedicated to my dear wife
Adelaide
Who waited patiently for me
during my eight and one-half years in the USA
preparing for the Gospel Ministry.

___CONTENTS___

____CONTENTS____

CONTENTS

Introduction,
A Synoptic Survey
of the Bible

The word Bible means "Book." Actually, it is a collection of books of the Old Testament written by the Jewish writers and the Gospels, Acts, the Epistles, and the Book of Revelation written by the Apostles of Jesus Christ.

The Bible contains 66 books: 39 in the Old Testament and 27 in the New Testament. The Old Testament books accepted by the Protestant Church as canonical are the same as the books accepted by the Jewish scribes.

At least forty different authors wrote the Bible during a period of approximately 1,500 years. The five books of Moses can be dated c. 1400 B.C. and the last book of the New Testament, Revelation, c. A.D. 90. In spite of the fact that the original manuscripts are now extinct, and that only handwritten copies existed up to the invention of printing, the condition of the text has been providentially preserved and remarkably kept pure in all ages.

The Hebrew Old Testament has been verified substantially by the LXX - The Septuagint, and by the Hebrew biblical manuscripts of the Dead Sea Scrolls which were discovered between 1947 and 1952. These manuscripts are in Israel's National Museum in Jerusalem today, dating in places back to the same period as the LXX. The existence of nearly 4,500 manuscripts of the New Testament in Greek, dating from c. A.D. 125 up to the invention of printing, provide a wealth of attestation to the New Testament. Added to this evidence are the various versions, such as the Old Latin and Syriac, going back to A.D. 150 and the Latin Vulgate translation made by St Jerome in Bethlehem (382 - 405).

The writers of the Bible represent men of all classes of society from shepherds, fishermen and tax collectors to prophets and kings. Yet, despite their different backgrounds and qualifications, the product of their writing is not a case of "many men of many minds," but of many men and one mind, that of God Himself. It was under the guidance of the eternal Spirit of God that they all wrote (2 Peter 1:21).

After having been prepared for their task by the providential ordering of their entire lives, the writers received, in addition to all that, a wonderful and supernatural guidance and impulsion by the Spirit of God, so that they were preserved from the errors that appear in other books. Thus the resulting book, the Bible, is in all parts the very Word of God, completely authoritative in its commands.

The all-wise God has revealed Himself to mankind even in His creation, but since that cannot teach man what to believe concerning God and the duty God requires of man, He has given us His Word. This Word reveals man's depraved condition and need, man's sinful and fallen condition, his inability to save himself, God's revealed will to save man through a substitutionary sacrifice (Isa 51:11-12; Heb 2:3-14), the salvation of man through saving faith alone (Eph. 2:8-10; Titus 3:5), and God's Covenant with Israel through Abraham to give them both a Saviour and a Kingdom.

This Covenant was expanded and developed in the ensuing covenants, namely the Sinaitic with Moses and Israel, and the Davidic. It was both expanded and fulfilled in the New Testament (Matt. 28:28; Heb. 8:6-13).

Types and antitypes

All the types given in the feasts, ceremonies, and sacrifices in the Old Testament, e.g., the Feast of Passover, typified Christ as our Passover and Sacrificial Lamb (John 1:25; Matt. 26:19; Heb. 9:28; 1 Cor. 5: 7). Christian baptism symbolizes the salvation which is in Christ and it is the antitype of the salvation which was offered in Noah's ark (1 Peter 3:21).

The greatest influence on mankind is the Bible. One of the great English poets, Coleridge, once said, *"To give a history of the Bible as a book would be little else than to relate the origin or first excitement of all of the literature we possess. From this storehouse of literary material our leading writers have most freely drawn."*

The world's greatest statesmen gladly credit the Bible with giving them whatever power they had with men. William E. Gladstone called the Bible, *"God's best and richest gift to mankind."* George Washington asserted, *"It is impossible to rightly govern the world without God and the Bible."* The author of the United States' Constitution, Thomas Jefferson, maintained, *"The Bible is the cornerstone of liberty."* *"Hold fast to the Bible as the anchor of your liberties,"* said Ulysses S Grant. Daniel Webster declared, *"I am profitably engaged in reading the Bible. Take all of this Book on reason that you can and the rest on faith and you will live and die a better man."* The prince of preachers, C. H. Spurgeon,

HE "a SAID thousand bucklers, all shields of mighty men." He went on to say that "If we want weapons we must come here for them, and here only. Whether we seek the sword of offence or the shield of defence, we must find it within the volume of inspired Scripture. If others have any other storehouse, I confess at once that I have none. I have nothing else to preach when I have got through with this book. I can have no wish to preach at all if I may not continue to expound the subjects which I find in these pages."

Finally, the chief influence of the Bible, as the Lord Jesus Himself said, is spiritual: "Search the Scriptures; for in them ye think ye have eternal life."

And so my dear readers and friends, the Bible is plain in the things that are necessary for your soul's needs, and God the Holy Spirit will make other things in it clearer as you read it. It is God's Book, not man's book. It is a message from the King of kings and Lord of lords. Study it, trust it, and live by it. Other books will deceive you but not God's Book - the Bible.

The
Old Testament

GENESIS

~

The Book of Beginnings

The first book of the Bible, Genesis, is the Greek title given to it in consequence of its subject matter. The name means "**beginnings.**" The two books in the Bible which the Devil and his followers particularly hate are Genesis and Revelation. The vicious attacks which have been constantly made upon them by infidels and critics down through the ages are because these books especially expose Satan and the subtleties of his host and predict his certain doom. Every Bible believer should therefore diligently study these marvellous books.

Queries concerning the origin of life and of things have always intrigued man's thinking. Discoveries of the past, as exhibited by the Dead Sea Scrolls and other archaeological discoveries in the Holy Land, not only challenge the scholar but fascinates the layman. Genesis provides an answer to man's inquiry into the past. Genesis records the beginning of heaven and earth, of all life - plant, animal and man; of marriage and family; of society and nations; of sin and crime; sorrow and death; of sacrifice and salvation.

The message in Genesis can be summed up In three great words, namely: generation, degeneration, and regeneration. In these words we have the beginning of the three worlds of nature, sin, and grace. They tell us what God did, that is, the creation of the universe and man in chapters one and two; what Satan did, that is causing the Fall and its consequences in chapters three through eleven; and in chapters twelve to fifty, what the God-man Jesus Christ will do. In fact, Genesis gives four clear identifying features concerning the Messiah: (1) As of the human race, (2) The Branch of the race by Shem (Gen 9:26), (3) The Nation of that Branch by Abraham (12:3) and (4) the Tribe of that Nation by Judah (49:10).

"In the beginning" introduces the developments in preparation of the universe for the creation of man. Whether this dateless point in time refers to God's original Creation or to God's initial act in getting the world ready for man, is a matter of interpretation. In either case the record begins with God as the Creator (1:1,2) in this brief introduction in accounting for the existence of man and the universe.

Man is immediately distinguished as the ultimate of God's entire Creation (2:4b-25). Created in God's image, he becomes the focal point of interest as the narrative proceeds. More details are given here about His Creation. God formed man out of the dust of the earth and breathed into his nostrils the breath of life, making him a living soul. Man was entrusted with the responsibility to care for the animals and was commissioned to name them.

The distinction between man and animals is further apparent in the fact that man was to have fellowship with his Creator and also that man found no satisfactory companionship until God created Eve as his helpmeet. Man was entrusted with the full enjoyment of all things abundantly provided by God in the Garden. There was only one restriction - man was not to eat the fruit of the Tree of the Knowledge of Good and Evil.

The most crucial period in man's relationship with God is the drastic change that was precipitated by disobedience (3: 1-24). As the most tragic development in the entire history of the human race, it is a recurrent theme of the Bible.

Genesis was not written primarily to teach science, but to explain man's need of a Saviour because of his sin and its consequences, and God's plan of salvation through a Saviour to be born of the *"seed of the woman."* Instead of contradicting true science, Genesis goes beyond the furthest reaches of science, and bridges the three great gaps which science-evolution cannot bridge, viz., the origin of matter, the origin of animal life and the origin of man. The significant words *"God created"* stand at each of these places where the evolutionist is put to confusion in his search for a *"missing link."*

Throughout the Bible there are references to creation and the early history of mankind portrayed in the introductory chapters of Genesis. How shall we interpret this account of the beginning of man and this world? Is it mythology, allegory, and contradictory combination of documents, or a single man's idea of the origin of things? Other biblical writers recognize it as a straightforward narrative God's activity in creating the earth, the heavens, and man. But the modern reader must guard against reading into the narrative, interpreting it in scientific terms, or assuming it to be a storehouse of information bearing upon recently developed ideologies. Interpreting this section of the Bible - or any other text, for that matter - it is important to accept it on its own terms.

When studying Genesis, it should be borne in mind that about 99 percent of the purpose of the book is to reveal the "WHO" of Creation and one percent to tell the "HOW" of Creation.

The ruin wrought by the entrance of sin into the world may be seen by placing together the first five words and the last four words of this book - "In the beginning God created" and *"a coffin in Egypt."* The coffin was a symbol of faith and hope through the Saviour who is the seed of the woman (3:15) and for whom the way is prepared in a chosen race descended from Abraham. He was to lay down his life for man (Mark 10:45).

Genesis closes with the great Messianic prophecy of Jacob, *"The scepter shall not depart from Judah, nor a lawgiver from between his feet, until Shiloh (Messiah) come; and unto him shall the gathering of the people be"* (Gen 49:10), and Joseph expressing his hope based on God's Covenant with Abraham. Joseph believed that God would fulfill His promise of bringing the children of Israel back to the Promised Land (Gen 15:1-21; 50:24-26).

EXODUS

~

The Going Out,
or Departure

Exodus is the second book of Moses. The English name for this book is derived from its Latin name Exodus, in turn from the Greek Exodus of The Septuagint, meaning the "going out or departure" (Exodus 19: 1).

Exodus is the great Old Testament book setting forth God's redemption. Its purpose is to describe how Israel became the Covenant nation of God. The concept of liberation from enslavement, idolatry and death is found throughout the book. Repeatedly God declares Himself to be Jehovah, His name as the Sovereign Deity making a covenant with Israel. He delivers them and brings them out of Egypt. He takes them to Himself to be His people and to be their God.

As Genesis ends with the picture of the "*coffin in Egypt,*" the introductory chapter of Exodus is connected with Genesis by the Hebrew conjunction "*and.*" It relates the national historic incident to carry the coffin of Joseph back to the promised land with the birth of Moses during the enslavement in Egypt. Exodus differs from Genesis in that its message concerns a nation, rather than individuals, and it may be summed up in three words, namely: **slavery, emancipation,** and **reconstruction.** In terms of geography, the three words would be: **Egypt, Red Sea, and Sinai,** which words suggest yet more: **The Ten Plagues, the Passover,** and the **Ten Commandments.**

The main character in Exodus is Moses. The history of Israel centers around the forty years of his preparation in the palace of Pharaoh and the further forty years of preparation as a shepherd in the very wilderness where the last forty years of his life in active national service would be spent in reconstructing a horde of slaves into a nation.

The ruler of this nation, however, was Jehovah; its constitution was the Law given on Mount Sinai; its national shrine was the Tabernacle; its bond of unity was the spiritual worship of the one and only true God, and its national hope was the *"prophet like unto Moses,"* (Jesus Christ: Deut. 18:15-18, Acts 3:2), whose blood would be shed for the spiritual emancipation of the Nation, as was that of the Passover Lamb (John 1:29), and whose bones, like those of the Lamb's should not be broken, who would come from heaven to be *"The Bread of Life"* for both Jews and Gentiles (John 6:51), as the manna was sent from heaven for the sustenance of the children of Israel during their forty years of wandering in the Wilderness of Sin.

Christ is the true Law-giver and Mediator of whom Moses was but a type. The work of salvation recorded in Exodus is only a fore-shadow of Christ's work of salvation (Heb. 9:24-28).

LEVITICUS

~

The Priest's Handbook

Leviticus is the third book of Moses. It was named by the Greek and the Latin versions because of its emphasis on the Levitical Priesthood. Ministers often turn to the Book of Leviticus for the order of service for such official acts as baptism, marriage, burials, etc.

The basic theme of Leviticus is "holiness," which word occurs more often in this book than in any other book in the Bible. The gap between God's holiness and man's holiness is wide. The Tabernacle, Sacrifice and Priesthood limit contact between God and His people to prevent the difference from becoming unbearable. Yet they do provide for the minimum of contact necessary to live within the Covenant.

The key verse to the book is in chapter 19:2: *"Ye shall be holy, for I, the Lord your God, am holy."* Atonement and rites of cleansing witness to God's willingness to remove elements inimical to holy fellowship. The law with its exhortations reveals God's will for His people to be truly holy in a moral sense as well.

The best commentary on Leviticus is the Epistle to the Hebrews, which explains its elaborate system of sacrifices and offerings in brief as follows:

"Without shedding of blood is no remission" (of sin) (Heb. 9:22).

In Hebrews we learn that these sacrifices and feasts, and the very priesthood of Leviticus were but a *"shadow of good things to come"* (Heb. 10: 1), and *"a figure for the time present."* Without Christ, our great High Priest, and the shedding of His own precious blood on the real Day of Atonement, Leviticus is meaningless.

When Christ died on the cross of Calvary, the Leviticus sacrifices were fulfilled and thus put away forever. The Holy of Holies in the Temple was to be entered no more with blood of bulls and goats, and so, as St. Mark said, *"the veil of the Temple was rent in twain from the top to the bottom"* (Mark 15:38).

Clothed with His righteousness, the holiness demanded in Leviticus is put within the reach of all the saved ones. *"But now the righteousness of God without the law is manifested, being witnessed by the law and the prophets; even the righteousness of God which is by faith of Jesus Christ unto all and upon all them that believe. . ."* (Rom. 3:21,22).

NUMBERS

~

The Book of Wanderings

The name of this book is derived from the two numberings of the children of Israel recorded in chapters 1-4 and 26, which were done in preparation for the military exploits on entering the *"promised land. "*

Numbers reveals God's love of order. Israel was not to be a mob but an orderly host. Each tribe and family and household had its allotted position and every man had his overshadowing cloud by day and by night.

This book should have been properly named, **"The Book of Murmurings."** They murmured against their Moses, the Priests, their food and drink, and against God. Their greatest failure came at Kadesh-Barnea when the twelve spies reported their findings after searching out the Promised Land. The majority report was one of pessimism and defeatism. The difficulties appeared insurmountable. They felt like grasshoppers in comparison with the natives of Canaan.

On the other hand, Caleb and Joshua rendered a minority report; they did not overlook the power of God as the others had done. They knew the God who delivered them from the hands of Pharaoh by making the Red Sea dry land for them, was well able to fight in their behalf.

The faithless Israelites yielded to their fears and refused to enter the *"Promised Land"* to whose borders God had already led them. The result of their unbelief was forty years of wandering and hard discipline in the wilderness until the entire adult generation which left Egypt, except Caleb and Joshua, had perished.

Numbers is highly supernaturalistic. This fact has prejudiced its case as untrustworthy in the minds of critics of the Bible. In addition to Israel being led (10:11-13) and cared for supernaturally (11:8, 9), there is the basic "**problem**" of the vast numbers of people involved; an army of more than 600,000 men, which implies that a nation of at least two million had to be sustained in the wilderness for nearly forty years. If this were an account of ordinary history, one could well question such a circumstance; but it is redemptive history, and its reliability is asserted by Jesus Christ Himself, the bread of life (Luke 24:44). There every argument should end.

Numbers teaches both the **goodness** and **severity** of God: **severity** in the punishment of sin, even the sin of Moses, God's appointed leader; **goodness** as shown in the daily supply of manna, and the guiding cloud, the water from the rock; and the brazen serpent for healing used by doctors today as a symbol of healing, which was but a type of Christ. "*And as Moses lifted up the serpent in the wilderness, even so must the Son of man be lifted up (on the cross); that whosoever believeth in Him should not perish, but have eternal life*" (John 3:14,15).

DEUTERONOMY

~

The Book of Instructions
or The Second Law

This is the last of the five books of Moses. The word **"Deuteronomy"** comes from the Septuagint title, deuteronomion, which means, repetition of the Law.

Ancient Jewish scholars as well as Christian writers unanimously attribute this book to Moses. Jesus Himself quoted from it (Matt. 4:4). Moreover, the various New Testament writers quote from it or allude to it nearly 100 times, often indicating that the citation came from Moses himself (Mark 12:9; Matt. 19:8; Rom. 10: 19; 1 Cor. 9:9). Modern critics deny that Moses wrote Deuteronomy, attributing its present form to various writers and editors over a period of centuries.

However, the fact that this book can be so identified confirms its own plain claims to its Mosaic authorship and the occasion for which it was produced (Deut. 1:3; 31:9-22, 24). By the same token it belies the modern higher critical theories of the origin of Deuteronomy.

Deuteronomy is not only the Moral Law expressed in the Ten Commandments, but also the Civil Law and the Ceremonial Law. It contains six farewell addresses of Moses, delivered within a period of 40 days immediately prior to his death.

The characteristic word of the book is **"remember,"** with which Moses summons memory to minister, to conduct and bring the influence of retrospection upon their prospect.

The first of these addresses from chapters 1-4 recounts the forty years of wandering, and warns against idolatry as their chief danger. God's providence is recounted to inspire obedience.

The second and longest address (chapters 5-28) explains the nature of the obedience demanded in the first address and pronounces the blessings of obedience and the curse of disobedience.

The third address (chapters 29-30), recites the Covenant in which God plights His troth with Israel and promises mercy and restoration when Israel shall repent of her violation of this truth.

The fourth address is found in chapter 31. It was delivered at Moses' one hundred and twentieth birthday celebration, in connection with which Joshua was prepared to succeed Moses. The Law was also rewritten for preservation by the Levites in the Ark of the Covenant.

Moses knew how religious and patriotic songs can inspire people. Those who will forget sermons often will remember songs; hence, in chapter 32, he sang a farewell song in his fifth address to gain the souls of the people and to remind them of their unfaithfulness to a faithful God.

The final address (chapter 33) is a blessing for the twelve tribes. The book closes with the scene of Moses ascending Mount Nebo to view the Promised Land and then to die.

Deuteronomy is valuable to believers because the Lord Jesus Christ approved it. He quoted three times from it to rout Satan in the Wilderness Temptation. In Deuteronomy *"all is love, yet all is Law."* This love and this Law both are fulfilled in Christ, of whom the book speaks so clearly as *"the prophet like unto Moses,"* whom God will raise up from the midst of the people (Deut. 18: 15, Acts 3:22-26)

JOSHUA

~

The Book of Possession

This is the sixth book of the Old Testament, and the first of the historical books. It was named after its principal character, Joshua. Under God's guidance he led the nation of Israel across the Jordan in their conquest of Canaan, in occupying the tribal territories, and in renewing their covenant of allegiance to the Lord.

In Jewish tradition Joshua is the first book of the prophets, the second major division of the Hebrew Bible, heading the sub-division known as the former prophets (Joshua, Judges, 1 and 2 Samuel, 1 and 2 Kings).

This book seems to have been written as the first official record of God's providential leading in Israel's triumphant settlement in the land He promised their forefathers. As such, the record was undoubtedly added to the existing scrolls of the Law and kept beside the ark in the Tabernacle (Deut. 31:9, 22-27).

The book falls into three major divisions, namely: (1) The conquering of the land, chapters 1-12; (2) dividing the land, chapters 13-22;- and (3) Joshua's farewell address, chapters 23, 24.

Whenever a national crisis arises, God is found ready with a leader thoroughly prepared, as was the case with Moses who was prepared for eighty years, forty years in Pharaoh's palace and forty years in the wilderness, to lead the children of Israel out of slavery in Egypt. Experience and training had prepared Joshua for the challenging assignment of conquering Canaan.

At Rephidim he led the Israelite army in defeating Amalek (Exod. 17:8-16). As a spy he gained firsthand knowledge of the existing conditions in Palestine (Num. 13, 14). Under Moses' tutelage, Joshua was trained for leadership and prepared for directing the conquest and occupation of the Promised Land.

The Book of Joshua is a book of war. It is a fearful story of the extermination of godless nations whose sins had become a stench. Israel was God's instrument for punishment of the Canaanites, just as later the Assyrians and Romans were tools in punishing the Jews for their disobedience and apostasy.

The fierce and bloody conflict was marked by the best military strategy, thirty-one kings and their tribes were defeated; but always in such a way that the children of Israel were reminded that their victories were not won by their power or might, but by the Captain of the Lord of hosts, who fought with them and for them. After the conquest of the land was completed, the land was divided by lots among the tribes for settlement.

Earlier an incident occurred in the book which lends color to much of the history of the twenty-five years it recounts. Rahab, the harlot, and her family were saved from the destruction of Jericho by a scarlet line which hung from her window. That crimson cord stands for the grace of God and salvation by faith alone, and the grace of God runs through all the Bible.

The Book of Joshua declares the faithfulness of

the Lord and of His covenant with the Patriarchs and with the nation. God is demonstrated as keeping His promises in full (Joshua 21:43-45).

The book closes with farewell addresses of Joshua to the people (chapters 23,24), in which he recounts God's mighty hand in their history and challenges them to choose Him as their God, the only God who had chosen them as His people: *"Choose you this day whom ye will serve ... but as for me and my house, we will serve the Lord"* (24:15).

This is the greatest need in today's world - true Christianity in the homes, the educational institutions, the restoration of the family altar by husbands; homes where honor is given to *"the Lamb of God who taketh away the sin of the world."* Jesus Christ is the only way, the truth and the life, who appeared to Joshua as *"Captain of the host of the Lord."*

An ounce of true Christianity in the homes and in the schools, is worth a pound of true Christianity in the church and society.

JUDGES

~

The Book of Declension

The book of Judges received its name from the thirteen judges whose deeds it records in the period of over three hundred years between the death of Joshua and the establishment of the monarchy under the first King. The most important of these Judges were Othniel, Ehud, Deborah and Barak, Gideon, Jephtha and Samson.

The book can be outlined as follows: (1) A historical introduction connecting its history with that of Joshua, chapters 1:1-3:6; (2) The history of the Judges, chapters 3:7-16:31, and (3) An appendix which reveals the awful spiritual and moral declension of the time, chapters 17- 21.

The era of the Judges was a period in which the Israelites as God's Covenant people were frequently in need of divine deliverance. Through Moses the Israelites had experienced release from Egyptian bondage as recorded in the Pentateuch. Under Joshua, the next generation partially conquered and occupied the Promised Land.

As subsequent generations succumbed to apostasy and idolatry which resulted in foreign oppression, they appealed to God for deliverance. Once more the mighty acts of God were displayed as the Judges responded to the call of God to lead the people in military exploits to rout the oppressing armies.

Thus, the purpose of this book in presenting history is definitely didactic, to teach divine retribution upon sinning, God's mercy upon repentance, and the futility of man-centered and idolatrous governments.

The book may be summarized as follows: (1) "*And the children of Israel did evil in the sight of the Lord*"; (2) "*And the Lord sold them into the hands of their enemies round about*"; (3) "*And when the children of Israel cried unto the Lord, the Lord raised up a deliverer who delivered them.*"

In the most deplorable fashion imaginable, these three phrases representing sin, punishment and deliverance, universally follow one another through sad political-religious cycles of history. God's people rarely bend to profit from their former sad experiences. The burned child persisted in rushing again into the same destroying fire of idolatry.

The Israelites' persistent declension in true spiritual worship is bound to their disobedience to God's command through Joshua. For instance, the corrupt people of the land "*utterly exterminated*" most of the tribes of Israel, yet Israel was guilty for her sad neglect in not utterly exterminating the inhabitants. They did not drive out the inhabitants but the Canaanites dwelt among them and became a constant thorn in the side.

It is the old story of "*marrying a drunkard to reform him.*" Israel was united with the Canaanite: and degenerated to the level of the worship of lust practiced by the heathen.

This book teaches us two outstanding lessons.

First, *"The wages of sin is death,"* and the only safety is in absolute separation from all evil. The second is that of the unfailing mercy and ready forgiveness of God when the sinner repents and cries to God for deliverance.

The Judges, or deliverers, in this book are all a type of the Lord Jesus Christ, our true Deliverer and Redeemer from sin and the punishments we deserve.

RUTH

~

The Book of Restoration

The beautiful character who is the heroine of the story, has not only lent her name to the book, but also to countless thousands of girls through the ages.

The story of Ruth is one of the choicest idylls of all literature; a love story that has fascinated millions and has lost none of its charm through the centuries.

We are introduced to the family life of the ancestors of King David in a simple and romantic form of historical narrative, which is in harmony with the tender and affectionate contents.

The story in this book is a classic among the stories of lovers because it contains the elements of profound sorrow turned into great joy; of love overcoming prejudice; of noble self-sacrifice richly rewarded in both hero and heroine; of true love sanctified by religion; of marriage and a life happy ever afterward.

Just as the story closes we catch a glimpse of a baby's crib, and hear the sweet music of a babe's cooing, in whose veins is running the blood of Israel's greatest King and of David's greatest Son, Jesus Christ, the Saviour of both Jews and Gentiles.

The widowed Naomi and Ruth and the noble Boaz stand out in sharp contrast against the dark background of the days of the judges which were bloody, immoral, idolatrous days, in which these noble souls lived by faith and faithfulness to God, and in love and purity in an evil generation.

So the story is a blow at pessimism, for even at its worst the world is not all bad. God always has his *"thousand who have not bowed the knee to Baal."* He has never and will never be left without a witness even though these be but *"a remnant."*

For the expression of loyalty and devotion, no human words have ever excelled these words of Ruth the Moabitess, to Naomi; *"Entreat me not to leave thee or to return from following after thee; for whither thou goest I will go; and where thou lodgest I will lodge: thy people shall be my people, and thy God my God"* (1: 16).

Here is supreme devotion, love to the uttermost. But its secret is kinship in the things of the soul: *"Thy God shall be my God."* There can be no true love without this kinship of the soul.

Scholars of the Bible differ widely as to the purpose of this book. However, it should be borne in mind that the author's primary purpose was to emphasize the providential care of God for two widows in desperate circumstances and, secondly, to show that the appearance and voice of David at a crucial period in Israel's history was not accidental. This evidence can be found in the closing note of the book about Obed, the child born to Boaz by Ruth; from whom sprang Jesse, the father of David. Thus, the Gentile Ruth became one of the physical forebears of the Lord Jesus Christ, who obliterates all race and class distinctions.

It is, therefore, not strange that among the four women mentioned in the genealogy of Christ in the first chapter of Matthew are included Rahab, the harlot; Bathsheba, the adulteress, and Ruth, the God-loving Gentile.

Truly, Christ is the Saviour of all men, regardless of race, nationality, or prestige. *"Though your sins be as scarlet, they shall be as white as snow; though they be red like crimson, they shall be as wool."*

FIRST SAMUEL

~

Three Biographies

1 Samuel is a book of transition between the theocracy established under Moses and the monarchy begun under Saul. It also marks the transition of national influence from the Priest to the Prophet. It is divided into the biographies of three men Samuel, Saul, and David. Samuel is second only to Moses among all the Old Testament characters. He is the last of the Judges and the first of the Prophets and the first to start a School of the Prophets. He is a tribute to the maternal influence of his godly mother, Hannah, in answer to whose prayer he was given.

As the Prophet of Jehovah, **Samuel** was to lead the people of Israel out of the times of the judges into those of the Kings. Consecrated like Samson as a Nazarite from his mother's womb, Samuel accomplished the deliverance of Israel out of the power of the Philistines, which had been only commenced by Samson, not by the physical might or power of his arm, but by the spiritual power of the Word of God and prayer; thus he led Israel from the worship of dead idols to the Lord its God.

The greatest grief of his life was that when he was old, Israel demanded of him: *"Make us a king to judge us like all the nations,"* whereas God wanted Israel to be a *"peculiar people"* unlike the other nations. God comforted him in the matter by assuring him that Israel had rejected Him rather than Samuel.

Saul, the next character, is one of the most **disappointing** individuals in the Old Testament. Never did a young man enter upon his life work with brighter prospects, and never did a youth so thoroughly prostitute his advantages. He was unappreciative of the wise counsellor he had in Samuel, unworthy of the noble son he had in Jonathan, untrue to the friend he had in David, and unfaithful to the trust of Kingship with which God honored him. His suicide in the battle of Gilboa is one of the notable tragedies of Scripture.

David, the final character, was God's choice for king rather than Saul. He was a man after God's own heart, the noblest of all the kings of Israel.

He was a man of war, but all his campaigns for the settlement of his Kingdom were waged in the same spirit in which as a youth he went forth to meet and slay the Philistine giant, Goliath: *"I come to thee in the name of the Lord of hosts, the God of the armies of Israel. . . ."* (1 Sam. 17:45).

The friendship of David and Jonathan is one of the brightest spots of the book, as the insane jealousy of Saul for David is the darkest spot. By that jealousy and the persecution and exile growing out of it, David developed into one of God's most noble men.

Thus, 1 Samuel records the story of the failure of earthly prophets, priests, and kings, which would be intolerably sad had it not been for the assurance that all these were but harbingers preparing the way for the coming, in the fullness of time, of Israel's ideal Prophet, Priest and King in the person of the divine Son of David, our Lord and Redeemer, Jesus Christ.

SECOND SAMUEL

~

The Rise and
Fall of David

2 Samuel might appropriately be named "*The Acts of King David.*" The first ten chapters tell of his glory as a King; the last fourteen chapters tell of his shame. There are no "white-washes" in the records of the Bible.

Repetitious chapters 1-4 outline the transition of the dynasty from the line of Saul to David. The rest of the book gives the events of David's reign; for example, his wars in chapters 10-12 and the rebellion of Absalom and its aftermath in chapters 14-20. David's royal thanksgiving hymn is recorded in chapter 22 (also in Psalm 18), but his death does not take place until 1 Kings 2. 2 Samuel ends with the purchase of the Jebusite Araunah's threshing floor as the proposed site for the building of the temple of the Lord.

The forty-year reign of David chronicled in this book is the golden age of Jewish history. One of King David's first official acts was to conquer Jerusalem and make it not only the civil but also the religious center of his great realm, bringing into it the tabernacle and the ark of the Covenant. His former capital was Hebron, where Abraham, Sarah, Isaac, Rebecca, and others were buried.

David would have gone further and built the temple had not God forbidden him to do so, and when forbidden to carry out this wish, he was obedient and generous enough to be a mere gatherer of the material and to allow another to have the honor withheld from him. His son Solomon had this honor, and this is a much needed lesson for us today.

Great and glorious as David was as a general, as a king and as the sweet Psalmist of Israel, he fell into the grossest and vilest of sins.

His sin of adultery with Bathsheba and his indirect murder of Uriah, her husband, represent the shame which, but for the grace of God, would have totally eclipsed his glory.

But no sinner was ever more genuinely repentant than David, or more ready to confess and admit the justice of the divine chastisement which fell upon him. Herein again he helps us in such songs for the penitent as he gives in Psalms 32 and 51.

Though repented and forgiven, David nevertheless suffered the consequences of his sin in the kindred sins of his own children, which broke their father's heart. This is a lesson which every man should learn. Surely, he who thinks that he can mock God and *"sow wild oats"* and not suffer in the time of reaping needs to read this second book of Samuel.

That such a sinner as David could, by genuine repentance, become *"a man after God's own heart"* is an encouragement to us. Moreover, the grace by which he was forgiven is still open to everyone in the glorious Kingdom of Christ, the Son of David and the Lord of David.

FIRST KINGS

~

The Story of Secession

The Book of Kings, which was but one book originally, was divided into two by the Alexandrian translators. They contain, in accordance with their name, the history of the Israelitish theocracy under the Kings, from the accession of Solomon to the extinction of the monarchy at the overthrow of the Kingdom of Judah, when Jerusalem was destroyed by the Chaldeans and the people were carried away into exile in Babylon, covering a period of about 455 years, from 1015 to 560 B.C.

First Kings covers a period of about one hundred and fifty years; from the death of David and Solomon's reign over the undivided Kingdom of the twelve tribes of Israel, when the Israelitish Kingdom of God stood at the summit of its earthly power and glory, though towards the end of this period the Kingdom began to decline. The rebellion of Solomon against the Lord in the closing years of his reign prepared the way for the rebellion of the ten tribes against the house of David. The book ends with the death of King Ahab, a period of shameful degeneration.

Solomon began well in seeking wisdom from God and in building a temple for God, unsurpassed for magnificence in all the architecture of the ages.

"Solomon in all his glory" is a phrase which represents the climax in material splendor which was bought at the expense of *"a grievous yoke"* upon the neck of his people, against which they rebelled upon the accession of his foolish son Rehoboam, who rejected the counsel of the elders.

The result was the secession of five-sixths of his Kingdom in the North, and thereafter causing the division of the Kingdom.

In the Northern Kingdom, Jeroboam, by the institution of calf worship, set the standard of wickedness and idolatry for a long chain of wicked kings who are described as *"doing evil continually in the sight of the Lord, walking in the way of Jeroboam, who made Israel to sin."*

No wonder God set such kings aside and made the Prophets the channel of His revelation and rule instead of the Kings. The great man of this period is Elijah the prophet, whom God raised up to check Ahab, the worst of all the Kings of Israel.

The curse of these times was the worship of Baal and Ashtoreth, which was adultery and the grossest immorality dignified by the cloak of religion, as is the case with much of the religious practices of the world today.

The mistake of the evil kings of both the Northern and Southern Kingdoms was their failure to realize that every king as a ruler of people is subject to God, and all earthly governments are under God. The late President Abraham Lincoln had this to say about the United States Democracy: *"Under God government of the people, by the people and for the people,"* and William Penn said, *"If you are not governed by God you will by tyrants,"* and finally Patrick Henry, that great patriot of America, said: *"It is when a people forget God, that tyrants forget their chains."*

Be it in a monarchy or a democracy, the ruler who overlooks that phrase *"this nation under God"* is a menace to good government. The kings and the kingdoms of this world must be subject to God and to the King of kings and Lord of lords (Rev. 19: 16). Any ruler who overlooks this fact will inevitably deny the liberty of the people he rules and will enslave them, like the Communist governments of this century. It should be borne in mind by every freedom-loving citizen as Thomas Jefferson put it, *"The God who gave us life gave us liberty at the same time. Can the liberties of the nation be secure when we have removed a conviction that these liberties are the gift of God?"*

SECOND KINGS

~

The Story of
Corruption and Captivity

2 Kings is the saddest book of all Jewish history; it is the book which records the carrying away into captivity of Israel by the Assyrians in 722 B.C. and the captivity of Judah which was begun by Babylon in 606 B.C.

Of the twenty-seven kings of Judah and Israel who reigned during the three centuries covered by this book, only six kings tried to serve the Lord and lead the people in the way of righteousness. All these six kings ruled in Judah, but even their reformations were short-lived, and the destruction of both kingdoms by their captors was God's judgment upon them.

The people's sin of idolatry and persistent rebellion against God was aggravated by the fact that this was the period during which nearly all of the great prophets of the Jews lived and preached, pleaded and prayed for Judah and Israel to return to the living God. For this was the "Elizabethan Era" of Jewish literature which gave to all ages the writings of Isaiah, Jeremiah, Hosea, Joel, Amos, Obadiah, Jonah, Micah, Nahum, Habakkuk and Zephaniah.

But the attitude of God's people toward the ministry and message of these prophets is expressed in the complaint of Isaiah, *who hath believed our report?*" How true this is with our generation.

Men may fail as Israel and Judah did to be a blessing to all nations, yet God cannot fail and will never fail. His purposes must prevail, if not in mercy, then in wrath. And so the period of the captivity came with the destruction of Jerusalem and the Temple.

This judgment forever purged Israel from idol worship. Whatever other sin Israel had after her return from the seventy years of captivity in Assyria and Babylon, idolatry was not one of them. They learned very well the lesson God sought to teach them when He made them again the slaves of idol-worshipping nations as in the case of the Egyptian bondage.

The remnant of the faithful souls who returned to rebuild Jerusalem and the temple at the decree of Cyrus in 536 B.C., were carrying forward the divine plan and preparation for the coming and the enthronement of Israel's true King and Saviour our Lord Jesus Christ. Isaiah said, *"His name shall be called Wonderful, Counsellor, The mighty God, the everlasting Father, the Prince of Peace"* (Isa. 9: 6b). The three wise men who came from the east at the birth of Christ asked Herod, *"Where is he that is born King of the Jews?"* (Matt. 2:2) and on the cross of Jesus at the crucifixion, Pilate wrote: *"This is Jesus the King of the Jews"* (Matt. 27:37). Jesus fulfills every ideal of Kingship so miserably lacking even in the best of Israel's kings.

FIRST & SECOND CHRONICLES

~

The History of the Temple

Apart from the books called "the prophetic-historic writings" - Joshua, Judges, 1 and 2 Samuel and 1 and 2 Kings which describe the development of the Kingdom of God established by means of the mediatorial office of Moses, from the time of the bringing of the tribes of Israel into the Promised Land, or until the Babylonian captivity, - the Old Testament contains five historical books: Ruth, Chronicles, Ezra, Nehemiah, and Esther. These latter stand in the Hebrew Canon among the hagiography.

The book of Ruth gives a charming historical picture from the life of the ancestors of King David. The Chronicles on the other hand, extend over a very long period of time in the historical development of the Israelite Kingdom of God. Then it embraces history from the death of King Saul until the Babylonian exile, and goes further back in the genealogies which precede the narrative of the history of Adam, the father of the human race.

From a comparison of the manner of representing the history in the Chronicles with that of the books of Samuel and the Kings, we can clearly see that the Chronicles did not purpose to portray the development of the Israelite theocracy in general, nor the fall and events which conditioned and constituted that development objectively, according to their general course. The Chronicles was interested in the portion of the history which relates to the temple and its services. Everything is seen from the priest's point of view rather than from that of the politicians.

The Chronicles were mainly interested in the history of Judah, and refers to the history of the Northern Kingdom only where it serves its purpose of throwing light on Judah and Jerusalem, and the temple. It emphasizes the reigns of the good Kings who reformed the religious life of the people and restored the service of the temple.

.The Chronicles deals in some detail with the reigns of David and Solomon, relating David's desire to build the temple and his preparation for it, and Solomon's building the temple.

Six chapters are devoted to the temple construction whereas only three chapters are devoted to all the other affairs of Solomon's glorious reign. The Chronicles makes room in its record for anything that concerns the priest or the temple services.

Despite his manifest preference to confine his writings to the record of the reforms, who cleansed the temple, restored the Law, or put away idolatry, the Chronicler is faithful in recording the wickedness of the King who led the people away from God's temple until their wickedness made it necessary for God to destroy the temple which the people had come to despise, and lead them away into Babylonian Captivity until their hearts should yearn again for God and the temple.

The Chronicler ends his records with the proclamation of Cyrus, King of Persia, which permitted the captives to return to Jerusalem to rebuild the Temple. So from the beginning to the end of 1 and

2 Chronicles, the writer never gets out of sight of the towers and pinnacles of the Temple. It could be said of him as it was said of Christ when later He cleansed the same temple: *"The zeal of thine house hath eaten me up."* To the Chronicler, this is God's story of His blessing upon those who seek first the Kingdom of God and His righteousness, and His judgment upon those who despise this law which Christ makes fundamental to true success and happiness.

EZRA

~

The First and Second Return from the Captivity

For the sake of making the number of books contained in the canon of Scripture correspond with the number of letters in the Hebrew alphabet, the Jews had from of old reckoned the books of Ezra and Nehemiah as one. The apocryphal book of Ezra is composed of passages from the second book of Chronicles. The books of Ezra and Nehemiah, and certain popular legends, had long been current among the Hellenistic Jews together with the canonical book of Ezra. Hence, this is how the book of Ezra is called Ezra in the catalogues of the Old Testament writings handed down to us by the church fathers.

Jeremiah prophesied the seventy years of captivity and the captives' return from Babylon. He did this by his parable of the vessel marred in the potter's hand and related how *he made it again another vessel.* The book of Ezra shows the divine potter remaking the Babylonian captives into a nation, making it possible for them to serve Him again.

The book of Ezra consists of two parts. The first part, comprising a period anterior to Ezra, begins with the edict of Coresh (Cyrus), King of Persia, permitting the return to their native land of the Jews in exile in Babylon, and ordering the rebuilding of the Temple of Jerusalem under Zerubbabel, chapters 1-6. The second part tells of a second group returning under the leadership of Ezra himself, and of his prosecution of the work began under Zerubbabel.

Since the first year of the rule of Cyrus corresponds with the year 536 B.C. and the seventh year of Artaxerxes

(Longimanus) with 458 B.C., it follows that this book comprises a period of at least eighty years. During this period there was an interval of fifty-six years, extending from the seventh year of Darius Hystaspis, (in which the Passover was celebrated after the dedication of the new temple [6:19-22],) to the seventh year of Artaxerxes, at which time Ezra went up with those of the second group.

The first responsibility of the first group of returning exiles was to restore the altar and all the offerings and feasts which they had shamefully neglected before the captivity.

The foundation of the temple was laid amidst weeping of the older generation, who had seen the greater splendor of the Temple of Solomon, and the joyous shouting of the younger generation.

The second contingent of captives returned under the leadership of Ezra, the Scribe, about eighty years after the first group under Zerubbabel. Ezra stands out as a great man of faith, so sure of the protecting hand of the Lord over the caravan of people and treasure that he was ashamed to ask the king for a military guard after professing faith in the protecting hand of God.

The conditions Ezra found in Jerusalem among the Jews who had returned earlier were distressing and demanded the drastic measures Ezra took to abate the evils, such as mixed marriages with the idolatrous neighbors.

The significance of the book of Ezra in sacred history lies in the fact that it enables us to perceive on the one hand, how the Lord so disposed the heart of the kings of Persia, the then rulers of the world, that in spite of all the machinations of the enemies of God's people, these pagan leaders promoted the building of His temple in Jerusalem and the maintenance of His worship therein. *"The King's heart is in the hands of the Lord..."* (Prov. 21:1).

On the other hand, He raised up His people, when delivered from Babylon, men like Zerubbabel their governor, Joshua the high priest, and Ezra the Scribe who, supported by the prophets Haggai and Zechariah, undertook the work to which they were called, with hearty resolution, under the powerful hand of God.

Thus, the temple sacrifices were restored, as the potter remakes a vessel. So there is hope for every soul marred by sin - the hope of becoming *"new creatures in Jesus Christ,"* who said, *"Ye must be born again."*

NEHEMIAH
~
The Third
Return from the Captivity

Nehemiah has long been linked with the name of Ezra in Hebrew Christian tradition. The book's close ties with I and II Chronicles in style and language, outlook and purpose, point to one work originally embracing Chronicles, Ezra and Nehemiah.

The extended use of personal memoirs from the hand of Nehemiah certainly makes him a substantial author of the material now bearing his name. The material comes from a document much like a personal diary. Some believe that Nehemiah never intended for it to be published, because the events and the emotions associated with it were reported very frankly and vividly. These first-hand observations are tremendously important in shedding light on the political history of the Jews during the Persian era.

Nehemiah, whose autobiography we have in this book, is one of the most admirable characters of the Old Testament, and one of the noblest patriots in Jewish history. His heart was broken by the reports that came to Babylon from Jerusalem telling of the desolation of the city of his father, its incompleted walls, its neglected temple and services and the afflictions of the remnant of Jews who had returned under Zerubbabel and Ezra.

Nehemiah's grief for his people won from King Artaxerxes the permission to lead back to Jerusalem a third group of captives (2: 1-6), about fourteen years after the return under Ezra.

So thoroughly did he imbue his countrymen with his patriotic zeal, faith and prayerfulness, that in a remarkably short space of time (fifty-two days), the colossal task of building the walls was accomplished for, inspired by him, *"the people had a mind to work."* This should be the attitude of Christians everywhere.

Of course, Nehemiah met with tremendous opposition from enemies in Samaria, led by Sanballat and Tobiah (4:1-3), but the work was pushed to completion with trowel in one hand and sword in the other. Nehemiah not only had to fight the ridicule and treachery of Samaria, but also the heartlessness of the "Loan Sharks" of his own people, who were enslaving their brethren by usury. *"The love of money is the root of all evil."* He rebuked them severely, shamed their greed by his own unselfish service and stopped their practices.

However, Nehemiah's restoration went beyond the material things of walls and gates and rates of interest. He restored the Word of God to the people in a true revival in which he had the cooperation of Ezra. The law of Moses was read and explained to the people and the people confessed their sin and entered into a Covenant pledging loyalty to Yahweh.

Repeatedly we see in this book the sense of right relation between faith and works expressed thus, *"We made our prayer unto our God, and set a watch against them day and night."* Nehemiah would have said with Cromwell, *"Trust in God and keep your powder dry."* Before God, he was justified by faith alone; before men he proved his faith by his works. *"Wherefore by their fruits ye shall know them"* (Matt. 7:20).

ESTHER

~

The Unfailing Providence of God

In the Hebrew Bible, Esther comes last in the group of five books bearing title Megilloth, following Ruth, Song of Solomon, Ecclesiastes, and Lamentations.

The Book of Esther is one of the most fascinating Books of the entire divine library. The scene is the court of Xerxes, King of Persia, during the eighty years' interval between the return of the Jewish captives under Zerubbabel and the return of those led back to Jerusalem by Ezra.

The book is sometimes criticized because it nowhere mentions God. However, it should be borne in mind that in a pagan atmosphere of hatred and opposition, it was not always expedient for the Jews to display their religion publicly. The Gentile populace resented the Jewish attitude toward idols, religion, foods, and mixed marriages. Thus without flaunting his religion, the author of this book conveys a spiritual emphasis.

Mordecai is shown to stand in the tradition of Shadrach, Meshach, and Abednego in refusing obeisance to Haman (3:2). His refusal is understandable only on the basis of his strict adherence to the Decalogue. Fasting is a further indication of Jewish religious practice (4: 16, 9:31).

The low state of morality at the Persian Court is revealed in the incidents against which the finer womanly sensibilities of Vashti rebelled, bringing about her removal from the throne.

About four years later, Esther, a very beautiful Jewish orphan girl raised by her cousin Mordecai, the keeper of the King's gate, was numbered among the virgins brought to Ashasuerus for the selection of a queen to reign instead of' Vashti.

The plot centers about Haman, the grand vizier of the Court, who hates Mordecai for refusing, as a Jew, to bow down to him, and in vengeance plots the massacre of all the Jews of the realm upon a given day.

Mordecai prevails upon Queen Esther, at the risk of her life, to break the precedents of the court by going into the King's presence unsummoned, to intercede for the life of her people. Esther's bravery and loyalty to her people is seen as she rises to the challenge in the noblest self-abandonment: *So will I go in unto the king, which is not according to the law: and if I perish, I perish"* (4: 16).

The outstanding religious motif behind this book is divine providence. The Jews learned under God's affliction what they would not learn under His forbearance. The author weaves the pattern of providence. Before Haman quarreled with Mordecai, Vashti's dismissal provided the occasion for Esther, a Jewess, to gain a position which enabled her to save her people. Mordecai had indebted himself to the King. Xerxes had a sleepless night at the right time and read in the right portion of the state records. All of this fits together. No Jew could have penned this without the intention of presenting the unfailing providence of God in the sparing of His people.

Haman's plot for the massacre of a race, his erection of a scaffold for the execution of Mordecai, his power behind the throne of a godless King, represents what James R. Lowell must have had in mind when he wrote:

> *"Truth forever on the scaffold,*
> *Wrong forever on the throne."*

But the thwarting of Haman's plot, the exaltation of Mordecai, the execution of Haman, and the salvation of the Jews, represent the overruling divine providence of the poet's next line:

> *"But that scaffold sways the future,*
> *And behind the dim unknown*
> *Standeth God amid the shadows,*
> *Keeping watch above His own."*

God's name need not occur in a book in which His might, power, and redeeming grace is vividly revealed, as He preserves the race through which, *"In the fullness of time,"* He has given His only begotten Son for the deliverance of mankind from the bondage of sin and death.

JOB

~

The Afflictions of the Rigtheous Man

Victor Hugo calls the book of Job, *"the greatest product of the human mind of all ages."* Certainly it is the sublimest dramatic poem in all literature. An English poet has this to say: *"Job, maintaining his virtue, and justifying the utterance of the Creator respecting him, sits upon his heap of ashes as the glory and pride of God. God, and with Him the whole celestial host, witnesses the manner in which he bears his misfortune. He conquers, and his conquest is a triumph beyond the stars. Be it history, be it poetry: he who thus wrote was a divine seer."*

There is no doubt that Job was a historical figure (Ezek. 14: 14; James 5: 11), but there is no way to ascertain exactly when or even where he lived except to say that it was probably in the desert of East Palestine and in the Patriarchal Period.

The author of the book of Job (probably one of the oldest books in the Bible) is unnamed and thus unknown, but whoever wrote it has been considered one of the most gifted dramatists in the history of literature. His purpose was not, as some believe, to illustrate the patience of a godly man, though that is surely involved, but to attempt to answer the age-old problem: **why do afflictions befall the righteous man if there is a God of mercy and love?** Thus, it deals with one of the oldest problems of the human race, why do the godly suffer?

Satan's sneer, *"Doth Job fear God for naught?"* could not be allowed to stand unchallenged. Therefore, Job's misfortunes are permitted by God for the purpose of vindicating Job's righteousness. From God's standpoint, Job's sorrows and ours are a testing; from Satan's standpoint, they are temptation.

Job's steadfastness under trial proved that he did not serve God for wealth, family or health, for he was deprived of all these, even of the sympathy of his own wife and friends, and yet he maintained his integrity, crying, *"Though He slay me, yet will I trust in Him."* Thus Job nailed the age-long lie, *"Every man has his price."*

Job's three friends, Eliphaz, Bildad, and Zophar, came to sympathize and stayed to criticize. Their philosophy is poured out upon the suffering in three rounds of speeches, to each of which Job replies in his own defense.

Their explanation of Job's suffering is that God is righteous and punishes only the wicked and blesses the righteous. In answer, Job voices a sentiment which still rises to vex many a sufferer, namely, that the righteous often suffer while the wicked (all those without God), seem to enjoy greater prosperity than the godly (the child of God). Jesus said, *"In the world ye shall have tribulation ... ."* (John 16:33b).

The more Job's friends argued, the more personal they became and (as it is still the case with this kind of religious argument), the less they accomplished. Instead of helping, they made Job's suffering worse.

Finally the voice of Elihu is heard as he speaks of the educational value of suffering and prepares the way for God to speak out of the whirlwind which by this time darkens the stage. This is the voice which Job and every godly sufferer longs to hear out of the storm of life.

Happy is the sufferer who can wait in patience until he hears God speak, and in whose life sorrow and pain have borne their wonted fruit in making God's voice audible and His commands sweet.

Thus, Job is vindicated and then turns about to minister to his friends. He does this, not after their method of argument and accusation, but by praying for them, thus again pointing to the importance of prayer. Our duty is to pray for the suffering saint, not to criticize him. Job's example has given great comfort and encouragement to the sorrow-stricken in all ages. However, the real man of sorrows is not Job, but the Lord Jesus Christ. He also furnishes the answer to all Job's questions, such as, *"If a man die shall he live again?"* He supplies Job's longing for a *"Daysman"* to stand between man and God and to lay his hand upon us, for His humanity touches man while His deity touches God, thus making a perfect *"atonement"* for man.

PSALMS
~
The Book of
Praise and Prayer

The Book of Psalms is a collection of Hebrew songs, hymns and poems taken from various periods in the history of Israel. The book itself furnishes no title, nor is such a title found anywhere in the Old Testament. The nearest approach to a title is found in Psalm 72:20: *"The prayers of David the son of Jesse are ended."* The later Jews gave the book the title *"Book of Praises."* The LXX entitled it *"The Book of Psalms"* out of which came the English title.

The Psalms not only stand exactly in the middle of our Bible, but they are the central shrine of worship for the saints of the Old Testament and the New Testament as well. They are not only the divinely inspired book of praise and prayer of the Old Testament, but they are as precious to the Christian as they are to the Jew.

The one hundred and fifty Psalms are clearly divided into five books, the closing of each book being marked by a doxology, namely: Psalm 41, 72, 89, 106, and 150.

Approximately half of the 150 psalms were written by David, whom we know had great artistic abilities (1 Chron. 13:8). A few Psalms were written by Solomon; by Asaph, one of David's court poets; by the sons of Korah, another group of professional writers; and one by Moses (Psa. 90). In addition, some of the Psalms are of anonymous authorship and were written over a period of many years.

The Psalms begin with a beatitude, as does the Sermon on the Mount. They appropriately rise to a great finale of praise in the group of songs known as the "Hallelujah Psalms."

There are several themes in the Psalms, and sometimes they are divided into groupings corresponding to these themes. For example, there are **penitential** psalms which pertain to repentance and sorrow for sin. The best of these is David's prayer for forgiveness after his sin of adultery with Bathsheba (Psa. 51). Others are Psalms 6, 32, 38, 102, 130, and 143.

There are also psalms called **imprecatory,** as they invoke the wrath and judgment of God upon the ungodly man. Psalms 5:10 and 139:21,22 have this element. However, it should be remembered that the poet is not expressing a desire for God's punishment of the wicked to satisfy his own feelings, but because he recognizes that the wicked have offended the honor of God.

Some of the most important sections of the Psalms are the Messianic sections which prophetically describe the future Messiah of Israel and His work. "The Royal Psalms" (2, 8, 45, 72,89,97, 110, 132) are so called because they depict Him in His regal splendor in which He will come as King to reign over His people. Others speak of the Messiah as the suffering One who must taste death before He can wear the crown. Among these are those referring to His betrayal into the hands of sinners (41 and 109), His crucifixion (22 and 69), and His bodily resurrection (16, 40, 66).

Hoary with age from two-and-a-half to three-and

a-half millenniums, the Psalms still have the freshness of the dew that fell this morning. The Psalms breathe worship in every note. Here it is confession, elsewhere it is supplication, again it is reflection, and anon, it is praise, but always it is worship, the bringing of every conceivable human experience into the presence of God, whether joy or grief, trust or anxiety, hope or despair. There are dirges written in minors and anthems pitched in majors.

There is no real possibility of anyone adequately analyzing the message of the Psalms for another; each soul must receive the message for itself and feel it as in the presence of God. One's favorite psalm, with the exception of the 23rd, which is always a favorite, depends upon his particular need at a given time.

In times of darkness and danger it is the 27th and 91st Psalms; in discouragement, the 34th or 86th; when seeking forgiveness, the 51st; when rejoicing over forgiveness, the 32nd; in times of joy, the 96th, 100th or 150th; when *down in the dumps*," the 110th; when thankful, the 98th, 102nd, or 194th. When we want to see God in His might, it is the 68th; when we want to see Christ in His glory, it is the 2nd or the 24th; fellowship with Christ in our sorrow, the 22nd; and when we are passing through the valley of the shadow of death, we turn to the 23rd Psalm.

The Psalms must have been the favorite part of Scripture even to our Lord and His disciples, for nearly two-thirds of the Old Testament quotations in the New Testament are from the Psalms. They found Christ in the Psalms at every point.

So in our generation, the songs that live are those that sing of Him and His grace. The best in music still centers about Him as in the Psalms. Christianity is of no doubt a singing religion, and the explanation is given by St. Paul in these words, *"Let the word of Christ dwell in you richly in all wisdom; teaching and admonishing one another in psalms and hymns and spiritual songs, singing with grace in your hearts to the Lord"* (Col. 3: 16).

PROVERBS

~

The Book of Wisdom

The name "proverbs" is taken from the first verse: *"The proverbs of Solomon the son of David, king of Israel."*

The Book of Proverbs, together with the books of Job and Ecclesiastes, constitute "the wisdom literature" of the ancient Hebrew people. It is claimed that this book was written by Solomon for the most part, and there is no argument otherwise. We know he was highly gifted in wisdom and literary talent (1 Kings 4:32), and that he wrote hundreds of proverbs and songs which have never been recovered.

The main purpose of this book is to reveal human wisdom or observation in the light of divine wisdom. The first nine chapters, addressed to *"my son,"* give us a series of parental counsels commending the virtues of wisdom and warning against the wiles of folly.

Proverbs treats such themes as wisdom, folly, sin, goodness, wealth, poverty, the tongue, pride, humility, justice, vengeance, strife, gluttony, love and lust. There is a comprehensiveness of outlook characterized by wisdom, so that no aspect of human relationship seems to have been overlooked. The tone is universalistic. The word "Israel" is not found in this book. Its teaching is therefore applicable to all men everywhere. However, the outlook is essentially in keeping with the Old Testament emphasis on Israel's hopes and material prosperity.

The key passage to the book is found in chapter 1: 7: *"The fear of the Lord is the beginning of knowledge,"* a saying so true and fundamental that it should be the slogan of, and emblazoned over the entrance of every school, from kindergarten to college and university.

The educator who ignores this fundamental principle has missed his calling; he should have been an animal trainer instead of instructor of human beings who have inherited a spiritual and moral nature from their Creator.

The ignoring of this essence of Proverbs on the part of many of those who make up the faculties of high schools and universities is doing a great harm to the students as well as to society. These ungodly teachers and educators are producing ungodly students who may become future leaders of their country. No doubt societies everywhere are morally and spiritually degenerating.

The book of Proverbs proves its divine origin in the fact that after three thousand years its counsels stand, unassailable by modern psychology and pedagogy. No one can successfully dispute the wisdom that says, *"Train up a child in the way he should go: and when he is old, he will not depart from it"* (22:6).

No better advice more needed by the youth of today can be given than Solomon's counsel in which he emphasizes the place of the home in child training. *"My son, hear the instruction of thy father, and forsake not the law of thy mother."* Or yet again, his wise counsel to the youth emerging from the home into the wider circles of companionship: *"My son, if sinners entice thee, consent thou not.*"

Parents who are reversing the commandment of Moses and obeying their children, might well heed the proverb, "*Chasten thy son while there is hope, and let not thy soul spare for his crying,*" or "*withhold not correction from the child: for if thou beatest him with the rod, he shall not die.*"

This is old fashioned counsel to many people, but our need of resorting to it will be vouched for by many who deal with those juvenile delinquents who have "enjoyed" too little of that sort of correction.

Whoever admires the wisdom of Solomon and yet heeds not the counsel of David's greater Son, Jesus of Nazareth, should heed this warning in Matthew 12:42: "*The queen of the south shall rise up in judgment with this generation, and condemn it: for she came from the uttermost parts of the earth to hear the wisdom of Solomon; and, behold, a greater than Solomon is here.*"

ECCLESIASTES

~

Is Life Worth Living?

This book is a treatise on a proper philosophy of life, and an outstanding example of Old Testament wisdom literature. No book of the Old Testament has suffered more at the hand of the higher critics than Ecclesiastes because of its alleged secular and pessimistic tone. Some feel it has no place in Scripture at all, a rather presumptuous opinion to say the least; others date it so late that it can scarcely be called Old Testament. After the discovery of the Dead Sea Scrolls and other ancient Jewish documents, the later idea is now discredited because it is recognized widely that Jewish literature from a very early period contained ideas similar to, but completely unrelated to, Greek concepts.

The book is basically a record of the reasoning of "man under the sun" or the secular man who lives without a recognition of God. If we look at the world without God, it appears what it is — a magnificent, graduated combination of diverse classes of beings, connected causes and effects, well-calculated means and ends. But thus contemplated, the world as a whole remains a mystery. If, with the atheist, we lay aside the idea of God, then, notwithstanding the law of causation, which is grounded in our mental nature, we abandon the question of the origin of the world.

If, with the pantheist, we transfer the idea of God to the world itself, then the effect is made to be as one with the cause, not, however, without the conception of God, which is inalienable in man, reacting against it; for one cannot but distinguish between substance and its phenomena. The mysteries of the world which meet man as a moral being remain, under this view of the world, altogether without solution. For the moral order of the world presupposes an absolutely good Being, from whom it has proceeded and who sustains it; it demands a lawgiver and a judge. Apart from the reference to this Being (God), the distinction between good and evil loses its depth and sharpness.

There is either no God, or all that is and happens in a moment is the being and life of God Himself, who is identical with the world. And so must the world's destructive power of sin remain unrecognized. The opinion as to the state of the world will, from a pantheistic point of view, rise to optimism; just as from an atheistic point of view, it will sink to pessimism. The view taken of the world, and the judgment formed regarding it, the book of Ecclesiastes, are wholly different.

The original name of the book was **Koheleth**, or *"the Preacher."* It was written by *"the son of David, King in Jerusalem."* The expression *"under the sun"* occurs repeatedly in the first few chapters and becomes the key to the real message of the book. Koheleth, Solomon, who had been king, sets forth the vanity of all earthly things from his own experience since his vision and desires are limited to things *"under the sun."* The striving after secular knowledge has proved to him unsatisfactory, trying one experiment after another in his vain search for something that will really satisfy his soul.

The result of every one of these experiments is

expressed in the plaintive wail *"Vanity of vanities: all is vanity."* Thus, in the spirit of a typical prodigal son in the far country of things *"under the sun,"* the King of Jerusalem seeks for satisfaction in a series of experiments in the realms of wisdom, pleasures, materialism, fatalism, pessimism, wealth and indifference.

All of these things' yield the same result of dissatisfaction, disappointment and vanity. Not until in chapter eleven does he tell us how he begins to get "out of the woods" where he can see that the things which satisfy do not come from *"under the sun"* but from *"above the sun."*

"How utterly futile, how utterly transitory, the whole thing is a puff of wind" (1:2; 12:8), is true of realistic humanism. Life without God has no meaning. Secularism can bring no lasting satisfaction. Faith, however, embraces the divine government.

The advice of this prodigal son, who finally came to himself and returned to his father, is *"Remember now thy Creator in the days of thy youth, while the evil days come not, nor the years draw nigh, when thou shall say, I have no pleasure in them."*

After giving us a most picturesque description of old age and life, he invites us to hear the "conclusion" to which all of his experiments have driven him; namely, that life is really worth living only to those who *"Fear God, and keep his commandments: for this is the whole duty of man."*

The Lord Jesus Christ expressed the same conclusion in this way: *"Seek ye first the kingdom of God, and his righteousness; and all these things shall be added unto you"* (Matt. 6:33).

SONG OF SOLOMON

~

The Course of True Love

The Song of Solomon is the most obscure book of the Old Testament and one of the world's most beautiful and dramatic stories of true love.

There are a number of inexplicable passages in the Bible which, if we understood them, would help to solve the mystery. The book is a love-poem. But why such a mini song in Scripture? This question gave rise in the first century, in the Jewish school, to doubts as to the canonicity of the book. Yet they firmly maintained it, for they presupposed that it was a spiritual and not a secular love poem. As such, they interpreted it allegorically, as the love between God and Israel or between Christ and the church which prevailed for centuries among Jews, Catholics, and Protestants.

The Song of Solomon is a story of a simple Palestinian girl, a Shulamite, from the vineyard of the north country. She was taken from her home and was to be one of the numerous wives of Solomon in Jerusalem.

But the maiden resists every effort on the part of Solomon to win her love away from the one to whom she plighted her troth, whose praises she sings to all about her in her waking hours and dreams of in her sleep.

Finally, after her true love has stood every conceivable test, she is allowed to return to her lover in her simple home. And so, by her faithfulness she rebukes the polygamy of any oriental court, resists the empty pomp and pageantry of the world, and proves the truth of the words of St. Paul in his wonderful classic on love: *"Love never faileth."* John, the beloved Apostle, said, *"There is no fear in love, but perfect love casteth out fear: because fear hath torment. He that feareth is not made perfect in love"* (1 John 4: 18).

In these days of marital unfaithfulness, resulting in an increasing evil of divorce when the ideas and ideals of the youth in the sacred matter of love are being molded so largely by secular ungodly novel writers and movie stars who at best are but *"blind leaders of the blind,"* there is a need of returning to the pristine purity of the love of the Shulamite and her rustic lover:

> For love is strong as death,
> Jealousy is cruel as the grave:
> The flashes thereof are flashes of fire,
> A very flame of the Lord,
> Many waters cannot quench love,
> Neither can the floods drown it;
> If a man would give all the substance
> Of his house for love,
> It would utterly be condemned.

The world is dying for a little bit of this kind of love — true love of this sort between husband and wife who know the meaning of marriage; true love between parents and child at home, and between neighbor and neighbor.

This sweet fragrance of the Shulamite's devotion to her lover has ever been regarded by the Jews to be a symbol of the relation between Israel and Jehovah. To the Christian, it symbolizes the faithfulness of the true Church, the Bride to the Bridegroom, Jesus Christ.

The Lord Jesus Christ is the true *"Rose of Sharon"* and the "Lily among thorns" and the church may sing of Him as fervently as did the Shulamite: *"His banner over me is love."*

This bridegroom *"loved the church and gave Himself for it."* He is gone to prepare a place for her. He will come again for His bride, and *"present it to Himself a glorious church, not having spot or wrinkle; but that it should be holy and without blemish."* In the meantime let the church be true to her divine lover, repulsing, as did the Shulamite, every attempt by Satan and his hosts to alienate her affections from Him to whom she is betrothed.

ISAIAH

~

The Gospel of the
Old Testament

The book of Isaiah is the first of the latter prophets (Isaiah, Jeremiah, Ezekiel, the Twelve) in the Hebrew Bible. Isaiah is regarded as the greatest of the prophets and one of the outstanding statesmen of the Jewish people.

The book itself gives only scanty information about Isaiah's literary activity. It is divided into two sections, not two books. Chapters 1 to 39 breathe the Old Testament spirit of judgment and warnings. Chapters 40 to 60 breathe the New Testament spirit of grace and peace.

In Isaiah's days the Kingdom of Judah was under five kings, both good and bad — Uzziah, Jotham, Ahaz, Hezekiah, and Manasseh. It was a sinful nation. Although the Israelites were God's people, yet they were apostate and deserved chastisement.

The conditions in Israel in Isaiah's day were a sad reflection upon God's people, yet strangely it is similar to conditions about us today.

The rich ground down the face of the poor. Their women were haughty and concerned chiefly with their false outward adornment. Religion had become an empty form devoid of spiritual matter. Like the modern social gospel, (St. Paul calls it another gospel, Galatians 1:8), the kings depended on their arms of flesh and despised the arm of Jehovah, their true defense.

Isaiah's eyes were not closed to the need of the poor

and the afflicted. With boldness and zeal he attacked the social ill of the day, not because he was a social reformer, but because he recognized these social abuses merely represented the terribly sick spiritual life of the nation (1:3-9).

The prophet became involved politically on a significant scale. Modern preachers must warn their governments against godless nations such as Communist countries. Stalin defined Communism when he wrote in his Problems of Leninism, *"Communist dictatorship means nothing more or less than the power which rests directly in violence, which is not limited by any laws (of God) nor restricted by any absolute rule."* This is a Satanic government and Christians must stand against it.

This was the time of the Pekah-Rezin coalition against Judah (735-732 B.C.). Ahaz decided that the only alternative he had was to appeal to Tiglathpileser III for assistance. Isaiah realized, however, that if Ahaz would quickly trust the Lord, the Syrian-Israelite alliance would come to naught (7:4). But Ahaz would not believe even when a special sign was given, so Isaiah had to tell him that the alliance would end in Assyria's domination of Judah.

Isaiah saw Jehovah as the real ruler *"sitting on a throne high and lifted up."* Yet he failed to make either king or people believe his vision. Even his prophecy of the Assyrian captivity of the Northern Kingdom and its sad fulfillment in his time made little impression upon those who heard the warning.

Isaiah calls the roll of all the surrounding enemy nations, Babylon, Assyria, Philistia, Moab, Damascus, Egypt, Arabia, and Tyre, and pronounces their doom and the reasons thereof, but still the people refuse to heed his warnings. The people of Israel rush on in their own destruction with a pace slackened only slightly by the reforms of the good King Hezekiah, whose faithfulness was rewarded by Jehovah's intervention against the hosts of the Assyrian invader Sennacherib.

In the second section of the book, Isaiah gives us the clearest Old Testament picture of the Messiah as the Servant of Jehovah. The heart of this section is the wonderful fifty-third chapter, which might well be called *"The Gospel according to Isaiah,"* with its clear picture of our Redeemer as *"despised and rejected of man; a man of sorrows, and acquainted with grief: ... he hath borne our griefs, and carried our sorrows: ... he was wounded for our transgressions, he was bruised for our iniquities."*

Isaiah gives us in his prophecy all the "fundamentals" of Christ's life which the New Testament later reveals to us, namely, His virgin birth (7:14); his descent from David (9:6,7 and 11:1); His vicarious atonement and continued life (chap 53); His second coming and final judgement (chap 61-66), and the closing glimpse of the new heaven and the new earth (chap 66:22; Rev 21:1,2).

It is no wonder, then, that when Philip found the Ethiopian eunuch riding his chariot and reading the book of Isaiah and desiring to have it explained to him, *"he began at the same scripture, and preached unto him Jesus"* (Acts 8:35).

JEREMIAH
~
The Weeping Prophet

Jeremiah consists of prophetic discourses, biographical materials, and historical narratives, though not arranged in strict chronological sequence.

It opens with the Prophet's call (chap. 1) and ends with the fall of Jerusalem (chap. 52).

Jeremiah was, however, more than a prophet. He was a statesman, a patriot and a martyr. His was a sad ministry accompanying a doomed nation to the death chamber for its execution.

Jeremiah prophesied during the reigns of the last five kings of Judah - the good King Josiah and his three wicked sons and grandson, Jehoahaz, Jehoiakim, Jehoiachin and Zedekiah. For half a century Jeremiah warned kings and people alike, with tears, of the doom and destruction which must come upon them for their persistent idolatry.

Despite this warning and the sad experience of the captivity of the Northern Kingdom in 721 B.C., they ended up with a like fate, and God raised up Nebuchadnezzar to destroy Jerusalem and the temple, and carry them into captivity in Babylon for seventy years. Jeremiah prophesied this captivity so clearly and repeatedly, for with all the nations, as well as with individuals, the *"wages of sin is death."*

Jeremiah is called *"the weeping prophet"* because of the way he poured out his soul in an effort to avert the captivity and destruction of his beloved people. But his message to King Jehoiakim was cut into pieces and burned in a fire, a treatment of the Word of God not greatly different from that accorded to it in some quarters today. In the Communist nations the Word of God runs counter to their willful and self-opinionated concept of a godless society which will lead eventually to self-destruction.

The Prophet was charged with treason and with weakening the hands of the defenders of Jerusalem. He was imprisoned and thrown into a filthy pit to die, but was rescued by friends.

The burden of the message is embodied in the vision given in the house of the potter. There, in the vessel of clay whirling on the wheel and marred in the hand of the potter, he saw the sad outcome of the Divine Potter's effort to make of his nation a vessel of beauty and usefulness. *"And the vessel that he made of clay was marred in the hand of the potter: so he made it again another vessel, as seemed good to the potter to make it"* (18:4).

This remaking of the marred vessel is the message of hope Jeremiah saw after the message of warning (Jer. 2:2, 3; 7:23; 11:2-5; 13:11). He preached it through tears. The message of hope presented the future restoration as a certainty. The political nation of Judah may perish, but the chosen people of God will survive. God will not utterly destroy His people but will bring them back after the seventy years. The eternal purposes of God will be realized in the record of the future glory (the book of hope, chapters 30-33).

The visible nation may fall, but true Israel will live on in the prophecy of the new covenant of grace and forgiveness of sins (31ff). Jeremiah equals the most evangelical section of Isaiah and other Old Testament prophets. His passionate love for his people and his desire for their salvation, his rejection by his own people whom he came to serve, his tears over the impenitence of Jerusalem and its destruction, reminds us of the greatest of all Judah's prophets, Jesus of Nazareth, Who, when He beheld the city, wept, saying: *"O Jerusalem, Jerusalem, thou that killest the prophets, and stonest them which are sent unto thee, how often would I have gathered thy children together, even as a hen gathereth her chickens under her wings, and ye would not! Behold your house is unto you desolate"* (Matt. 23:37,38).

LAMENTATIONS

~

The Bible "Crossword"

In Lamentations we have Hebrew poetry at its best. It consists of five separate poems, similar in style, all bemoaning the horrors of the destruction of Jerusalem and the suffering of the Jews brought about by the overthrow of the city by the Chaldeans under Nebuchadnezzar.

In the Hebrew Bible the literary form of the poems are acrostics and each verse in the stanza begins with the Hebrew alphabet. Of the five chapters, chapters 1, 2, 4 and 5 have twenty-two stanzas, the number of the letters of the Hebrew alphabet, and chapter 3, three times this number. The meter peculiar to the Hebrew elegy characterized the book - the long line and a slow, solemn movement. This same peculiar form of Hebrew poetry is found in the 119th Psalm and other Psalms and Proverbs.

The poetry of Lamentations is also to be noted in the balancing of contrasted ideas in its lines throughout. The dirge effect is secured by the weakening or shortening of the second part of the line, producing the musical effect of a crescendo followed by a diminuendo.

As a matter of fact, the Bible, judged from a literary point of view is unexcelled among the literature of all ages, to say nothing of its primary moral and spiritual ministry to the soul of the devout reader who searches the Scripture to find in it everlasting life.

The message of Lamentation which Jeremiah presented with his own tears is that *"the way of the transgressor is hard,"* and *"the wages of sin is death."*

He vindicates the righteousness of God's judgment upon the ruined city and its stiffnecked inhabitants: *"For the Lord hath afflicted her for the multitude of her transgressions;" "Jerusalem has grievously sinned, therefore is she removed;" "The Lord is righteous; for I have rebelled against his commandment."*

But despite the fearfulness of the lament over the siege of Jerusalem, when, because of its famine, *"the hands of pitiful women have sodden their own children"* and *"made their meat in the destruction of the people,"* the weeping prophet is never without hope or assurance of God's merciful purpose in their punishment: *"This I recall to my mind, therefore have I hope. It is of the Lord's mercies that we are not consumed, because his compassions fail not. They are new every morning; great is thy faithfulness. The Lord is my portion, saith my soul; therefore will I hope in him"* (3:21-24).

Jeremiah laments not simply because Jerusalem is destroyed and the people devastated; but rather that the catastrophe is God's act, executing merited punishment. Those who should have been the responsible leaders have not led aright, and the people have willingly followed. God is punishing Israel for its sin. But the adversity is not only punitive, it is also corrective. God's Covenant love and purpose have not failed.

To Jeremiah, even in this funeral dirge, notes of joy, hope and comfort have their place, for as the Lord Jesus said in the Sermon on the Mount, *"Blessed are they that mourn; for they shall be comforted."*

EZEKIEL

~

The Exile Prophet of Hope

Ezekiel is one of the major prophetic works of the Old Testament and it bears the name of the prophet whose divinely inspired messages and visions are recorded in it.

As Isaiah is the statesman prophet of faith and Jeremiah the martyr prophet of love, Ezekiel is the exile prophet of hope.

The theme of the book is the glory and transcendence of the Lord. The Jews in exile must realize that their God has not been defeated by the heathen powers but is justified in judging His own people, and that He is not limited to divine activity within the confines of Palestine, but is present with them in far away Babylon.

The scene of Ezekiel's entire ministry was the Babylonian Empire where he was carried with the second group of captives eleven years before the captivity was completed in the destruction of Jerusalem.

Ezekiel uses more symbolism and allegory than any other Old Testament prophet. His figures of speech are not dependent on heathen sources but have their foundation in the sanctuary of Israel and in the concepts of his predecessors.

Ezekiel shaped a type of prophecy known as apocalyptic. It is characterized by the frequency of visions and emphasis on the future or eschatological period with its tremendous catastrophic movements and direct interventions from heaven.

The book is divided into two major parts separated by a collection of foreign oracles. The division is based on the news of the siege and fall of Jerusalem (24:1,2; 33:21). Chapters 1-24 make up the first division and in the main, contain denunciations of the wickedness during the reign of Zedekiah, the last King of Judah. The second division, chapters 33-48 is occupied with promises to the future remnant of Israel.

The first twenty-four chapters recount Ezekiel's call and prophecies. During these early years he sought in vain by his numerous parables and impersonations to convince his fellow exiles of the coming destruction of Jerusalem and the righteousness of God's judgment in destroying it.

The pageantry of his miniature siege of Jerusalem is represented in the title bearing the picture of the doomed city; the shaving of the prophet's hair and beard and the burning and cutting and casting to the winds of the three parts of the hair, symbolizing the fate of the inhabitants of the city; the prophet's enactment of fleeing exiles escaping from the hole in the wall with few personal effects; and his bereavement at the sudden death of his wife, for which he was commanded not to mourn. These are but a few of the incidents of the prophet's ministry which make this book one of the richest in imagery in the divine records.

At any time he pronounces the doom and destruction of Jerusalem and pictures the horror of it all, the prophet vindicates the justice of God in the punishment of the people for their gross sins of idolatry and impurity, and repeatedly affirms the purpose of God, that by punishment the suffering people may learn to know Him, repent, and be saved. For no phrase occurs more often in this book than the words, *"And ye shall know that I am Jehovah."*

Yet it is sad to say that all of this ministry of Ezekiel fell upon deaf ears. The exiles refused to believe that Jerusalem would fall until one of the refugees came with the sad news, *"The city is smitten."*

In the meantime the prophet pronounced the doom of the seven surrounding nations which had oppressed God's people, repeatedly indicating the purpose of this judgment also in his most familiar phrase, *"They shall know that I am Jehovah"* (chapters 25-30).

After the news of the destruction of Jerusalem reached the exiles, Ezekiel's ministry met with more favorable reception, and from chapter 33 to 48 we have his great gospel of hope in which he prophesies the restoration of God's ancient people to all their former glory.

The nation of Israel which is like a valley full of dry bones shall live again; the ancient temple is seen restored and filled with the glory of the Lord which the prophet, in his earlier visions, had seen depart from it. The altar and its offerings are restored and the prophet sees a great river of the water of life proceeding from the temple to bless the world.

Ezekiel closes his book with a picture of the same heavenly city described by the beloved Apostle John in the Revelation, and names the city *"The Lord is there."*

How wonderful it is that this clear vision of the gospel of hope which is fulfilled in the Lord Jesus Christ, the "Prince" of Ezekiel's prophecy, should have come forth from the darkest hour of Israel's national history, the Babylonian captivity!

Truly, *"Night brings out stars as sorrow shows us truth - we never see the stars till we can see naught but them. So with truth."* The writer of Hebrews put it this way, *"Now no chastening for the present seemeth to be joyous, but grievous: nevertheless afterward it yieldeth the peaceable fruit of righteousness unto them which are exercised thereby"* (Heb.12:11).

DANIEL

~

The Book of Revelation
of the Old Testament

An Old Testament hero, Daniel is the main character of the book that bears his name. Of noble or royal birth (Dan. 1:3), he was taken captive to Babylon by Nebuchadnezzar in 605 B.C. with other Jewish youths of like ability and attainments (1:1-7), where he spent the remainder of his life and gained distinction as statesman and prophet.

Though Daniel lived during the Babylonian exile, yet it was not, as in the case of Ezekiel, in the midst of his countrymen, who had been carried into the captivity, but at the court of the ruler and in the service of the state.

Although of a despised subject race (Israel), Daniel rose to a position of dominating influence under four Kings of three different nations — Nebuchadnezzar and Belshazzar the Chaldeans, Darius the Mede, and Cyrus the Persian.

Daniel's youthful courage of conviction regarding the king's meat and wine and his willingness in later life to be cast into the lion's den rather than change his custom of prayer to Jehovah were not isolated incidents of his life, but rather fair samples of the stuff of which he was made: *"Train up a child in the way he should go: and when he is old, he will not depart from it"* (Prov. 22:6).

His interpretation of Nebuchadnezzar's dream of the colossus with head of gold, breast and arms of silver, belly and thighs of brass, legs of iron and feet of iron and clay is the most wonderful panorama as of world history ever given to the human mind by its

Creator. From Daniel's interpretation of the vision (chapter 2), together with that of the vision of the four beasts, the lion, bear, leopard, and the fearful fourth beast (chapter 7), and the vision of the ram and the rough goat (chapter 8), it is known that the head of gold represents the Chaldean Empire, the breast and arms of silver the Medo-Persian Empire, the belly and thigh of brass the Grecian Empire, and the leg of iron the Roman Empire, and the feet and ten toes of iron and clay, the various world powers which will come under the revived Roman Empire.

The significant part of the vision is the marvelous predictions of the coming of the Messiah and the Kingdom of God. *"The stone cut out of the mountain without hands,"* which represents the Kingdom of Christ, shall smite the composite image of the anti-Christ and destroy it and then increase into a mountain filling the whole earth.

This is God's plan whereby *"the kingdom of this world are become the kingdoms of our Lord, and of his Christ"* (Rev 11:15).

Another vision of Daniel whose fulfillment is still in the future is that oF *"the seventy weeks"* recorded in chapter 9. One has to read Revelation 11-19 to get a clearer picture of what is recorded in this section of Daniel.

These "weeks" are weeks of years or seven years and are divided into three periods: (1) the *"seven weeks"* or forty-nine years which saw the restoration of Jerusalem three score and two weeks (62 weeks) or 434 years "*Unto the Messiah the Prince,*" that is, to the time of Christ, and (3) "*one week*" or seven years, a period still in the future, which will usher in at the events attending the second coming of Christ.

When this "*seventieth week of Daniel*" will begin, Christ said, "*No man knoweth, not even the angels in heaven, but my father only.*" But one of the signs of the end time, Christ said would be "*the abomination of desolation spoken of by Daniel the prophet.*" Both Daniel and Christ Himself prophesy His "*Coming in the clouds with power and great glory*" (Dan. 7:13, 14; Matt. 24:30).

The Lord Jesus said of this day, "*It is not for you to know the times or the seasons, which the Father hath put in his own power.*" So, we are not to set dates for His second coming, but be ready at any time to meet Him at his coming with joy and not with trembling. Meanwhile, Christ said, "*Occupy till I come*" (Luke 19:13).

HOSEA

~

The Brokenhearted Prophet

The book of Hosea is the first of the *"Minor Prophets"* in the English Bible and the twelfth in the Hebrew. The book bears the name of its author, and is the sole source of information about Hosea's life and ministry. However, more is known of his home life than of any other prophet, since it was the basis for his message to God's people.

Hosea was a contemporary of Amos in Israel and Micah in Judah. His prophecy is the only surviving writing from the northern prophet to his own people, although Amos, a Southerner who ministered to the Northern Kingdom, has a book in the sacred Scriptures.

The book falls into two parts: the prophet's domestic life (1: 1-3: 5), and the prophetic discourses (4: 1-4:9). The period of his prophecy, 775-715 B.C. was one of great prosperity under King Jeroboam II, but one of great corruption of moral and shameful political conditions, four of the seven kings of his time having been murdered by those who succeeded them.

No prophet was ever more a part of his message than Hosea. His unhappy domestic life with his unfaithful wife, Gomer, was not only a preparation for his ministry, but a parable to the nation of its spiritual adultery in forsaking Jehovah and resorting to the worship of a false god, Baal.

The broken-hearted prophet loved Gomer in spite of her persistent sin and life of shame, and even after her lovers abandoned her to be sold, Hosea found her and forgave her all and took her again as the wife of his love.

Through his own grief God's messenger was prepared to understand the grief of Jehovah concerning the spiritual adultery of His people and to know the infinite love that made God willing to follow after Israel to win His people back to love and faithfulness.

The keynote to his message is found in chapter 4:1; *"For the Lord hath a controversy with the inhabitants of the land, because there is no truth, nor mercy, nor knowledge of God in the land."* For this condition Hosea is unsparing in his denunciation of kings, priests and people. Then, as now, it was a case of *"like priest, like people."* The priests even encouraged sin that they might profit more from the offerings of the people. Similar situations exist in our time today. Gay pastors are being ordained into the ministry and unbelieving rich men are put in places of authority in the church of God.

Such mockery is an abomination to God, for *"he desired mercy and not sacrifice; and the knowledge of God more than burnt offerings."*

Hosea, by his clear prophecy of the Assyrian captivity as God's punishment for its idolatry, attempted to do for Israel what Jeremiah later attempted to do for the Southern Kingdom of Judah. But his warnings fell on deaf ears, and the nation rushed on to its own destruction within five years from the time that Hosea's voice was stilled.

Truly, *"Ephraim was joined to idols"*; he was a *"cake not turned"* (half baked), and yet God loved these people as passionately as Hosea loved the unworthy and unfaithful Gomer.

And when Israel's destruction seemed inevitable, the heart of God sobbed out, *"How shall I give thee up, Ephraim? How shall I deliver thee, Israel? Mine heart is turned within me, my repentings are kindled together. . . . O Israel, thou has destroyed thyself; but in me is thine help."*

The book closes with a final appeal to the prodigal nation and a promise of mercy: *"O Israel, return unto the Lord thy God,"* and *"I will heal their backsliding, I will love them freely."* This God will do for every sinner who repents of his sins and accepts His Son Jesus Christ as his Saviour.

In Amos there is portrayed the unapproachable righteousness of God, while in Hosea there is demonstrated the unfailing love of God. Just as Luke writes of the prodigal son, so Hosea tells of the prodigal wife.

JOEL

~

The Prophet of Pentecost

Joel cannot be identified with any other Old Testament person bearing this name, and nothing is known of him outside of the book. But his name (Jehovah is God) expresses his message, and so it is usually taken as historical.

Joel was one of the earliest of the prophets of Judah probably exercising his ministry near the time of Elijah and Elisha, at the turn of the eighth century (ca. 800 B.C.).

His message is directed to Judah and has as its theme "The day of the Lord." This expression appears frequently in the prophetic books. It speaks of the time of divine judgment and has many connotations. For instance, it may speak of a historical day of judgment, or a period of judgment, or even of an eschatological day or period of reckoning. At the time all of these may be in the mind of the prophet as he looks down through the years, and may not be able to distinguish exactly in his mind what fulfillment he sees.

The keynote of his prophecy is found in chapter 1: 15: *"Alas for the day! for the day of the Lord is at hand, and as a destruction from the Almighty shall it come."*

Joel made vivid the desolation that God would send upon Judah and Jerusalem by likening God's destroying hosts to a scourge of locusts which probably at that time was spreading desolation and famine through the land, cutting off the food supply of man and beasts, and making it difficult to secure even the sacrifices necessary to maintain the temple services.

In the shadow of the judgment of this *"day of the Lord,"* Joel pleaded with priest and people alike to turn to the Lord in genuine repentance, saying, *"Rend your heart and not your garments, and turn unto the Lord your God: for he is gracious and merciful, slow to anger, and of great kindness,"* a message so needed today.

Joel prophesied not only the things which were near at hand, but also the things which were not fulfilled until about eight hundred years after, as well as the things which are not yet fulfilled, but will be fulfilled at the final judgment attending the second coming of the Lord Jesus Christ.

The Apostle Peter took one of these prophecies of Joel's as his text for his sermon on the day of Pentecost, which he said was fulfilled in the outpouring of the Holy Spirit on that day. *"This is that which was spoken by the prophet Joel: And it shall come to pass in the last days, saith God, I will pour out of my Spirit upon all flesh: and your sons and your daughters shall prophesy, and your young men shall see visions, and your old men shall dream dreams: and on my servants and on my handmaidens I will pour out in those days of my Spirit; and they shall prophesy"* (Joel 2:28-32; Acts 2:16-21). The complete fulfillment of this prophecy will be at the second coming of Christ.

Thousands of souls were saved in that Pentecost sermon through repentance and faith in the Lord Jesus Christ, the only way, truth and life. Those who have not yet found this salvation should heed the solemn words of Joel, where he says of them, *"Multitudes in the valley of decision: for the day of the Lord is near in the valley of decision."*

AMOS

~

A Layman
Preaching Judgement

Amos was a prophet, a speaker for God, but not of his own choosing, because he denied being either *"a prophet or a prophet's son."* His comprehension of the spiritual scene of his day had led many to classify him as the beginning of a new order of prophets.

His ministry led him to Bethel, the center of religious apostasy in the Northern Kingdom (1 Kings 12:26-33). The last years before the fall of the Northern Kingdom were characterized by great material prosperity. The people still enjoyed the luxury of military victories during the reign of Jeroboam II. Israel put temporal security above her trust in the living God.

The burden of Amos is national accountability for national sins. God will bring every nation on the face of the earth into judgment for its attitude toward Him and its treatment of humanity. Accordingly, Amos pronounces the judgment of God upon six surrounding Gentile nations for the national sins that had characterized them. Finally, he dealt with greater severity with the sins of Judah and Israel, because they had sinned against greater privilege and clearer light, Jehovah and His Laws.

The keynote of his message is found in chapter 3: 1, 2, *"Hear this word that the Lord hath spoken against you, O children of Israel, against the whole family which I brought up from the land of Egypt, saying, You only have I known of all the families of the earth: therefore I will punish you for all your iniquities."*

Amos' denunciation of Israel can serve as an outline

for study of social, moral, and religious conditions of people everywhere. Socially, two distinct classes had developed; the poor and the rich. The rich were seeking greater riches by any means (2:6, 7). Moral evils were rampant. Drunkenness and sexual license which were at an abominable level (2: 7, 8), speak of drugs and sex movies of this century.

Religious perversion was at a gross high, like the current ecumenical movement which is uniting all religions for a one world church. In Israel, idolatry was common (2:8). The faithful were scorned, chastised and mocked (2: 12). So are those who are standing faithful to God and His Word in our day, because they will not compromise.

The depth to which the people had fallen is characterized in their seeming indifference to their position as a delivered and cared-for nation (2:9-11). Repentance and obedience were imperatives, the only way to escape from imminent judgment.

Amos' bold challenge to the nation was: *"Prepare to meet thy God, O Israel"* (4: 12). To enforce his warning he pictured the coming destruction of the nation in five visions of judgment, namely: the locust plague and fire sweeping the nation, the plumb-line showing its crookedness, the basket of perishable fruits symbolizing its decay, and the spiritual famine of God's withdrawal from the nation.

It is no wonder that Amos' prediction came to pass within fifty years in the captivity and destruction of the Northern Kingdom by the Assyrians.

The book closes with a promise to *"raise up the tabernacle of David that is fallen, and close up the breaches thereof,"* to *"raise up his ruins"* and *"build it as in the days of old."*

In the book of Acts, chapter 15:15, 16, James the Apostle quotes this promise of Amos and claims its fulfillment in the Lord Jesus Christ and His Church made up of both Jews and Gentiles.

OBADIAH

~

The Doom of Edom

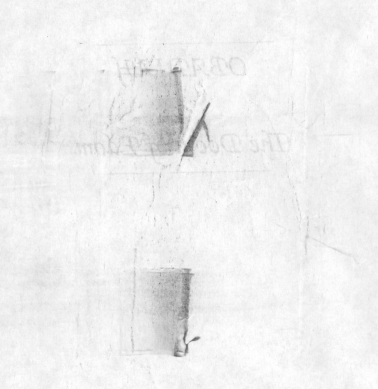

The oldest and briefest of the prophecies is the Book of Obadiah. Obadiah may be contemporary with Elisha, because of the theme of the book. He predicts that Edom would be destroyed by the Lord for having failed to assist Judah, his brother, in a time of need (2 Chron. 21: 16-17).

To understand Obadiah, one must know the age-long conflict between Esau and Jacob, the progenitors of these two hostile nations of Edom and Israel.

The very name *"Edom"* meaning *"red"* reminds us of the mess of red pottage for which Esau sold to Jacob his birthright which he despised (Gen. 25:20-34). Edom, therefore, stands for all the forces that hold spiritual things in contempt and despise God.

The Edomites dwelt in the rocky passes south of Judah and felt that no God was necessary for their protection. Today the ruins in Petra, Jordan, testify of this rocky dwelling place of the Edomites. They hated Israel because Israel worshipped Jehovah. The Communists, like the Edomites, are haters of Israel and the worshippers of Jehovah.

Upon Israel's return from Egypt, Edom had refused them passage through their borders. Today thus, Obadiah, in order to warn the Edomite against this policy of vindictive hatred, prophesied the way in which they would gloat over the destruction of Jerusalem and its captivity.

The keynote to his message is found in verse 15,

and is applicable to any individual or nation today as it was to Edom of old: *"For the day of the Lord is near upon all the heathen: as thou hast done, it shall be done unto thee: thy reward shall return upon thine own head."*

A greater than Obadiah expressed the same eternal truth in the words: *"With what measure ye mete, it shall be measured to you again"* (Matt. 7:2).

In all this age-long conflict between the forces of God and the Devil, between Edom, representing carnalities, and Israel, representing spiritualities, the battle may go on now and then; however, the ultimate outcome is sure. God will triumph over evil, the Spirit over the flesh, Jacob over Edom, and Christ over the Devil and his anti-Christ.

"But upon Mount Zion shall be deliverance, and there shall be holiness; and the house of Jacob shall possess their possessions... And there shall not be any remaining of the house of Esau: for the Lord hath spoken it" (vv. 17, 18).

Yet in this solemn warning of Edom's judgment, the way of escape is pointed out by Obadiah in his closing words. An Edomite may still repent of his sins and be saved through the Saviour who came through the Jews and is coming back to Mount Zion. *"And saviors shall come up on mount Zion to judge the mount of Esau; and the kingdom shall be the Lord's"* (v. 21).

King Herod the Great, an Edomite, tried to slay the new-born King of the Jews, but he failed, and to his son and successor the Lord Jesus sent this message, *"Go ye, and tell that fox, Behold I cast out devils..."*

King Herod the Great is in no sense either great or kingly in comparison with the real King of kings he sought to destroy. For as Obadiah says in his closing words of triumph, *"The Kingdom shall be the Lord's."*

JONAH
~
The Elder Brother of the Prodigal Son of the Old Testament

Jonah is fifth among the writings of the twelve minor prophets. He was an early contemporary of Hosea and Amos in the Northern Kingdom of Israel in the prosperous days of Jeroboam II (2 Kings 14:25).

Unlike the rest of the twelve, this book is entirely a historical narrative and not at all a collection of oracles. As a matter of fact, the only prophetic utterance in the book is *"Yet forty days, and Nineveh shall be overthrown"* (3:4b). Only the fact that Jonah was recognized as a true prophet can account for its inclusion in the canonical book of the twelve.

The parish God assigned Jonah was not among his own people, but in the hated city of Nineveh, the capital of Assyria, to warn the great metropolis of God's impending doom upon it.

Jonah preferred to "demit the ministry" rather than to go and preach to the Ninevites, whom he did not care to see saved. Therefore, he sought to evade the call, and set sail for Spain. He was swallowed up by a great fish (chapter 2), this being God's method of teaching him the impossibility of escaping the presence of Jehovah.

Jonah in the belly of the fish is often considered to be the biggest problem in the Bible. The frequent mistake of Bible scholars is to be too preoccupied with proving the fish-swallowing by historic parallels. While survival of such an experience is well documented relative to sperm whales, it is unnecessary, since chapter 1:7 makes it clear that *"the Lord had prepared a great fish."*

There are also the miracles of Nineveh's repentance and of the gourd. All these are involved in a complex of miracles. The reliability of any miracle depends upon God to perform them and not of man to explain them. Jonah prophesied close to the time of Elijah and was a contemporary of Elisha in the Northern Kingdom, whose contacts with Phoenicia (1 Kings 17:9-24) and Syria (2 Kings 5) were likewise accompanied by many miracles.

The Lord Jesus testifies of Jonah in reference to his death and resurrection (Matt 12:38-41; 16:4). This fact was not accepted by Jesus alone, but by the Scribes and Pharisees to whom He commended the event as a sign.

The book of Jonah is the greatest foreign missionary sermon of the Old Testament. Jonah was a typical Jew of his day. Foreign evangelism was not the principal mission of Israel as a chosen people. Furthermore, Jonah had no sympathy with God's plan to save this wicked heathen city. And when this prodigal city repented at his unwilling preaching and the Father rejoiced over their repentance and saved the prodigal city, Jonah did exactly what the elder brother in Christ's parable of the prodigal son did. *"He was angry and would not go in."* Pouting in his booth overlooking the city, he even criticized the love that forgave the repentant returning prodigal. *"But it displeased Jonah exceedingly, and he was very angry. And he prayed unto the Lord, and said, I pray thee, O Lord, was not this my saying, when I was yet in my country? Therefore, I fled before unto Tarshish: for I knew that thou art a gracious*

God, and merciful, slow to anger, and of great kindness,
and repentest thee of the evil" (4:1, 2).

In contrast to the angry pouting prophet overlooking the repentant heathen city of Nineveh, is that of Christ overlooking the unrepentant city of Jerusalem: *"When he was come near, He beheld the city, and wept over it."* Christ's parable of the prodigal son was spoken to rebuke those of every age who have the spirit of Jonah, which exemplifies the self-righteous elder brother who had no joy over the return of his prodigal brother (Luke 16).

MICAH

~

The Champion of the People's Cause

Nothing about the circumstances of Micah's life is known other than what may be gathered from his writings. According to these, he no doubt prophesied in Jerusalem, the capital of his native land.

It might be said of Micah, as it was said of the great prophet of whom he writes, *"the common people heard him gladly."* Micah was a contemporary of Isaiah in the days of Kings Jotham, Ahaz, and Hezekiah of Judah.

The book consists of three prophetic addresses which are clearly distinguished from one another in form by similarity of introduction (all three commencing with "Hear," chapters 1:2; 3: 1; 6: 1), and substantially by their contents.

Micah, *"the champion of the people's cause"* was against all kinds of evil practised by social and religious leaders, who oppressed and wronged the people. He bitterly denounced the princes who, as he put it, *"hate the good, and love the evil; who pluck off their skin from off them, and their flesh from off their bones;"* who *"abhor judgment and pervert all equity."*

Micah was severe in his arraignment of the false prophets who made his people err, *"who divine for money,"* and who prophesied peace or war to the people, depending upon whether or not they were well-paid.

He rebuked the dishonest merchants who enriched themselves by their *"scant measures," "wicked balances"* and *"deceitful weights."*

For all these oppressors of his people he boiled down his ideal of true religion in the words, *"to do justly, and to love mercy, and to walk humbly with thy God."*

Micah was truly the *"commoner"* of his day, the champion of the common people against those who wronged them politically, economically, and religiously. His teaching applies to the oppressors of the common people today.

His clear prophecy about the destruction of Samaria and its captivity came to pass within his own time. But Micah had a vision of a better day, a day of universal peace and goodwill to men. He saw the coming out of the *"little town of Bethlehem"* a ruler in Israel who would be a special prophet, priest and King.

The Scribes, in answer to King Herod and the wise men's question, turned to Micah's prophecy in chapter 5:2, where Christ should be born: *"But thou, Bethlehem Ephratah, though thou be little among the thousands of Judah, yet out of thee shall he come forth unto me that is to be ruler in Israel; whose goings forth have been from of old, from everlasting."*

So Micah becomes the prophet we especially love to hear at Christmas time. He, like Isaiah, his contemporary, tells us of the child born and a Son given, who is to be called, *"The Prince of Peace. Of the increase of his government and peace there shall be no end. . ."* (Isa. 9:6, 7a).

Micah says of the Christ born in Bethlehem, that this man shall be the Prince of Peace. *"He shall judge among many people, and rebuke strong nations afar off; and they shall beat their swords into plowshares, and their spears into pruninghooks: nation shall not lift up a sword against nation, neither shall they learn war any more. But they shall sit every man under his vine and under his fig tree; and none shall make them afraid"* (4:3,4).

Such a vision and hope are indeed *"good tidings of great joy . . . to all people."* No wonder that at the birth of this *"Prince of Peace"* the angels said, *"Glory to God in the highest, and on earth peace, good will toward men."*

NAHUM

~

The Doom of Nineveh

Nahum is the seventh book in order of the Minor Prophets and is the second division of the Hebrew Scripture. The Septuagint places it immediately after Jonah since both inveigh against Nineveh, the capital of Assyria.

The theme of the book is the judgement upon Nineveh for her sins of pride. The theme is well expressed in chapter 1:2 - the Lord takes vengeance on His adversaries.

About 200 years after Jonah had preached to the city of Nineveh and threatened it with destruction, as a result of which the city repented and was spared, the prophet Nahum was called to pronounce the doom and destruction of Nineveh for *"repenting of its repentance."* From Scriptural accounts, amply corroborated today in the excavation of the ancient city of Nineveh, it is certain that Assyria and Nineveh, its capital, represented the utmost in all the forces opposed to God. Nineveh was at the height of her power and glory when Nahum wrote to comfort Judah for her fear of what this cruel power might do to her.

The prophet's name, which means *"consoler"* or *"comforter"* is indicative of his message to his people in their fear of this *"blood city"* as he calls it. It is a stern, hard message of doom for a city that had sinned against God. The key verse of the book is found in chapter 1:2, 3. In the words, *"God is jealous, and the Lord revengeth; the Lord revengeth, and is furious; the Lord will take vengeance on his adversaries, and he reserveth wrath for his enemies. The Lord is slow to anger, and great in power, and will not at all acquit the wicked. . . ."*

As Nineveh sowed, so must she reap. This is the lesson Nahum has for men and nations today. The destruction to come was good news to Judah and to any other nation that feared Nineveh, for *"The noise of a whip, and the noise of the rattling of the wheels, and of the prancing horses, and of the jumping chariots. "*

This gospel of deliverance Nahum sang to Judah in the words, *"Behold upon the mountains the feet of him that bringeth good tidings, that publisheth peace!"* (1:15).

From St. Paul's use of this text in Romans 10: 15, we know that the destroyer of our spiritual Nineveh, the tyrant and the oppressor of God's people, is Satan. But the Lord Jesus Christ is the only One that bringeth tidings that publisheth peace.

HABAKKUK
~
The "Job" of the Prophet

Nothing is known about Habakkuk apart from the book that bears his name. Very likely he witnessed the decline and fall of the Assyrian Empire, and it is very likely that he was aware of the rising power of the Babylonians when this message was revealed to him.

If the patriarch Job and the prophet Habakkuk had ever met, they would have become bosom friends like David and Jonathan. The problem of both men was why a just and omnipotent God at times permits the evil doer or the wicked to flourish and the righteous to suffer affliction at their hands.

In Job's case the problem was personal, while that of Habakkuk was the affliction of the people of God (the nation that perplexed). Herein lies the peculiarity of Habakkuk among the other prophets. While the others plead with the people in behalf of God, Habakkuk pleads with God in behalf of the people.

The uniqueness of this book is apparent in two distinctive features. First, Habakkuk records his dialogue with God in which he raises theological problems and listens to the answer. In addition, chapter 3 is a psalm with musical terms noted in the first verse and the last verse.

Habakkuk asked why God should allow the unspeakable Chaldeans to afflict the people of God, the nation of Judah. Learning that the Chaldeans were merely a tool of God's using for the purpose of disciplining Judah for her own shameful cruelties and idolatry in the days of the wicked King Manasseh and

Amon, the perplexity of the prophet is only intensified, for why should the nation which was chosen to scourge be so immeasurably worse than the nation to be scourged? The solution to this problem is found in the key passage of the book (2:4), *"Behold, his soul which is lifted up is not upright in him: but the just shall live by his faith."*

Granted that the Chaldean is haughty, and intoxicated with power and the most wicked of nations (typical of Communist Russia and her allies), nevertheless the righteous who wait patiently through the affliction in faith shall live, and live more abundantly than the wicked who oppress them.

No message is more needed in our time than this one. It should be emblazoned on billboards, as God told Habakkuk, *"Write the vision, and make it plain upon tables, that he may run that readeth it."*

In the midst of life's problems those who make "snap" judgments of God whose mysteries they don't understand are apt to cry out with Habakkuk, *"The wicked doth compass about the righteous; therefore wrong judgment proceedeth."*

By faith he discloses to the righteous that:

Behold the dim unknown,
Standeth God within the shadow
Keeping watch above His own.

Therefore, faith's more mature counsel is given

through Habakkuk in these words, *"But the Lord is in his holy temple: let all the earth keep silence before him"* (2:20).

Thus by faith he rises,
To the height of this great argument
To assert eternal providence
And justify the ways of God to men.

Job found his way through the same mysteries of affliction and cried, *"Though he slay me, yet will I trust him."* So, *"the just shall live by faith."* This is St Paul's text for his two great Epistles to the Romans and Galatians and the 16th Century Reformation was based on the same text. The Lord Jesus said, *"Whosoever liveth and believeth in me shall never die."*

ZEPHANIAH

~

The Prophet of Judgement

Zephaniah prophesied in the 7th Century B.C. in the days of Josiah. He was the son of Cushi and a descendant of Hezekiah (1: 1), probably the King of Judah. Because of his royal lineage, he was able, with impressive force, to rebuke the sins of the princes (1:8).

Zephaniah's message is chiefly concerned with the coming great and terrible *"day of the Lord."* For over half a century during the reigns of the wicked Kings Manasseh and Amon, idolatry and all manner of wickedness had gone unrestrained and had all but exterminated the worship of the living God.

Little wonder that the prophet saw in the ravages of the Scythian lords, pouring down upon the neighboring nations, a harbinger of the fearful judgment that Judah deserved for her sins, and which she was to receive in the *"day of the Lord."*

The keynote of his message is found in chapter 1: 12. *"And it shall come to pass at that time, that I will search Jerusalem with candles, and punish the men that are settled on their lees: they say in their heart, the Lord will not do good, neither will he do evil."*

When God is thus ignored by princes and those who claim to be prophets and common people, there is a need of their being warned of what Zephaniah called *"a day of wrath, a day of trouble and distress, a day of wasteness and desolation, a day of darkness and gloominess, a day of clouds and thick darkness"* (1:15).

This preaching is unpopular for any age, but nonetheless wholesome and necessary. Zephaniah, like Amos, prophesies the doctrine of judgment to fall upon the surrounding Gentile nations. But he goes further than any other Old Testament prophet in his vision of the conversion of the Gentile to the worship of Jehovah. He is broad enough also not to demand that they come up to Jerusalem for their worship, but says, *"Men shall worship him, every one from his place, even all the isles of the heathen."*

In this forward look into the universal and spiritual true worship, Zephaniah is not excelled until the Lord Jesus said to the Samaritan woman, *"Woman, believe me, the hour cometh, when ye shall neither in this mountain, (Gerizim) nor yet at Jerusalem, worship the Father. But the hour cometh, and now is, when the true worshippers shall worship the Father in spirit and in truth: for the Father seeketh such to worship him"* (John 4:21,23).

No other prophet pictures judgment darker than Zephaniah, neither does any paint a brighter scene than the sunburst in 3: 15 as he sings of the glories of the Messianic Kingdom of Jesus Christ: *"The Lord hath taken away thy judgments, he hath cast out thine enemy: the king of Israel, even the Lord, is in the midst of thee: thou shalt not see evil any more."*

HAGGAI

~

The Temple Building Prophet

Haggai was a post-exile prophet. References to Haggai outside of the book bearing his name are Ezra 5:1 and 6:14. His name means *"festal,"* from the Hebrew word *"hag,"* meaning *"festival."* Possibly he was named by godly parents because he was born on some major Jewish feast day.

Haggai and Zechariah, his contemporary, were both among the party of Jewish exiles who returned from the Babylonian captivity with Zerubbabel in 536 B.C.

Immediately upon their return, they restored the altar of Jehovah and its sacrifices and laid the foundations of the temple. Then came the opposition of enemies, the discouragement of the builders, and the abandonment of the work for fourteen years, all of which we read about in the book of Ezra.

The book may represent merely an outline of his messages. The Lord had spoken through him to stir up the people to a successful effort to rebuild the Temple (1: 12-15). The condition at this time is vividly reflected in his approach to the people. Although they were deeply engaged in private housing projects, the prophet is a messenger of God to inspire the people to complete the Temple, reminding them that the Lord of hosts was the controller of the material blessings which they were lacking through drought and crop failure (1: 2-11).

Haggai's messages consist of four addresses, all delivered within about three months, in the year 520

B.C. The key passage to his message is found in chapter 1:8: *"Go up to the mountain, and bring wood, and build the house; and I will take pleasure in it, and I will be glorified, saith the Lord."*

The people were attempting to hide their indifference to the interests of God's house behind the pretense that *"the psychological moment"* for temple building had not yet come. *"The time is not come, the time that the Lord's house should be built."*

Haggai's first objective was to shame the people into immediate action by contrasting their own *"ceiled houses"* with the heap of ruins that marked the site of God's house.

Soon the pendulum swung to the opposite extreme. The people, who for years were satisfied to have no temple, were now dissatisfied because the temple they were building was not to be as glorious as Solomon's Temple, which some of the oldest of the exiles had seen.

God, through Haggai, assured them that the glory of this latter house should be greater than the former, because *"the desire of all nations shall come and I will fill this house with glory."*

The builders then began to barter for increased prosperity because of their piety represented in their temple building. And like the Apostle Peter they were saying, *"We have left all and followed thee; what shall we have therefore?"*

Haggai's third address was to correct this mercenary spirit by reminding them of the years of defilement of their sins and counseling them to wait more patiently for God's blessing.

From the day he uttered his final address to quiet their fears of the surrounding nations and their armies, they were to look to God as their defense, for he had promised, *"I will shake the heavens and the earth."*

The writer of the Epistle to the Hebrews (12:26-28) quoted this text and applied it to what the Lord Jesus Christ is yet to do when He comes to replace the kingdoms of the earth with the Kingdom of Heaven that cannot be shaken.

ZECHARIAH

~

The Prophet of the Last Days

Zechariah is recognized as the prophet of comfort, hope, and glory. He was a contemporary with Haggai and associated with Zerubbabel in the rebuilding of the temple in the discouraging years following the return from the Babylonian exile.

The book opens on the ethical note of the need of repentance and a full return to the Lord. Then follows a series of eight night visions. Zechariah deals almost exclusively with the Jews and as such it should be studied by all who are inclined toward anti-semitism to reveal what glorious plans God has for Israel. It shows a day coming when *"ten men shall take hold out of all languages of the nations, even shall take hold of the skirt of him that is a Jew, saying, We will go with you, for we have heard that God is with you."*

And so, those who hate the Jew and would persecute him because he is a Jew should read Zechariah and *"watch their step!"*

The eight visions in the first eight chapters were given to the prophet to strengthen the people in circumstances which would have been disheartening but for the hope of victory he showed them afar off.

The vision of the four horns and four *"carpenters,"* or carvers, raised up to destroy them, stands for nations that have oppressed the Jew and the instruments chosen of God to discipline these nations.

The vision of the measuring line predicts a new Jerusalem that cannot be measured of God. The vision of the candlestick represents Israel supplied with the Spirit of Christ enlightening the world. The vision of the flying roll represents the future reign of divine Law throughout the world. The vision of the ephah represents the final restraint to be put upon the evils of commercialism. The final vision of the four chariots represents the administration of Jehovah through the crowning of the true Joshua and the Branch, the Lord Jesus Christ.

Zechariah was strong for faithfulness in the completion of the restored temple, and reformation from the sins which necessitated the former destruction and captivity. Therefore, his key note is found in 1:3, *"Thus saith the Lord of hosts; Turn ye unto me, saith the Lord of hosts, and I will turn unto you, saith the Lord of hosts."*

The last six chapters contain a marvelous portrayal of the first and second advent of Christ. In the first advent Zechariah reveals the humiliation, suffering and death of the Lord Jesus, all fulfilled in our Redeemer, in His triumphant entry into Jerusalem, the betrayal for the thirty pieces of silver, the disposal of the blood money for the potter's field; the piercing, the wounds in His hand and the cleansing fountain, thus opened for sinners in the house of David.

Zechariah gave us a marvelous picture of Christ's second advent in great glory to set up His Kingdom on the earth. Apart from Isaiah, no Old Testament prophet gives us such a picture of Christ and no other is so repeatedly quoted in the new Testament.

His vision into the glories of the future Kingdom is excelled only by that granted to St. John six hundred years later on the Island of Patmos and recorded in the Revelation, which is an echo of the book of Zechariah.

MALACHI

~

Conceited Failures

Malachi is the last of the Hebrew prophets, as well as the last book of the Old Testament. The books of Malachi and Nehemiah should be read together, because they form respectively the last pages of Old Testament prophecy and history, born of the same social and religious corruptions and at almost the same time.

Malachi ministered about four hundred years before Christ, and a few years after the close of Nehemiah's ministry. His prophecy represents a call to Israel for repentance and obedience with a stern warning of judgment on the disobedient and the rebellious. He places considerable emphasis on the day of the Lord (3:2, 17; 4: 1, 3, 5), closing the Old Testament with a final promise of the Messiah.

Both Malachi and Nehemiah dealt with the priests, defilement of their office, the people's defilement of the home through mixed marriage with idolaters, and the general contempt for and neglect of the offerings and services of the house of God.

The key that unlocks his message is the word "wherein" which is found seven times in the book, in as many impudent and arrogant replies of the people in which they deny the prophet's charges against them: *"Wherein has thou loved us?"* (2: 17); *"Wherein have we despised thy name?"* (1:6).

"Wherein have we polluted thee?" (1:7); *"Wherein have we wearied him?"* (2: 17); *"Wherein shall we return?"* (3:7); *"Wherein have we robbed thee in tithes*

and offerings?" (3:8); *"Wherein have we spoken against thee?"* (3:13). Thus the people entered a general denial to all the prophet's charges of religious, moral and social corruption. In their self-righteousness they were utterly unconscious of any fault in the matters for which he rebuked them.

Truly, this was the darkness of spiritual night, but it was that darkness which preceded the dawn. The first faint streaks of that dawn are indicated in Malachi's prophecy of Christ's near approach, preceded by his forerunner, John the Baptist: *"Behold, I will send my messenger, and he shall prepare the way before me: and the Lord, whom ye seek, shall suddenly come to his temple, even the messenger of the covenant, whom ye delight in: behold, he shall come, saith the LORD of hosts.* (3:1)

From his mountain top of prophetic vision, Malachi sees the full glory of the approaching sunrise, and with a joyous shout announces it to the people lying in darkness: *"Unto you that fear my name shall the Sun of righteousness arise with healing in his wings"* (4: 2).

After four hundred years of oppression and cruelty suffered by the Jews at the hands of various world powers, this prophecy of the rising of the Sun was fulfilled in the coming of Him who said, *"I am the way, the truth, and the life." "I am the light of the world."*

The
New Testament
of our
Lord & Saviour
Jesus Christ

MATTHEW

~

The Story of
Jesus Christ as King

The Bible does not contain "four Gospels," for there is only one Gospel of Jesus Christ, and this "good news" is related by four different evangelists Matthew, Mark, Luke, and John — all writing to different nationalities to portray Jesus Christ from four different standpoints.

Matthew, a Levi and a tax collector or publican whom Jesus called to be one of His disciples, wrote the first Gospel to the Jews to prove to them that Jesus of Nazareth was the King of the Jews and that the Messiah of Jewish prophecy and ritual of the Jews was fulfilled. True to his purpose of convincing his fellow Jews that Jesus was their Messiah, he traces His genealogy, not from Adam, as Luke does, but from Abraham, the great father of the Jews.

Although Matthew is strongly Jewish in its character, it was written also for the benefit of Gentiles. The final commission enjoined the twelve apostles to make disciples of *all the nations* (28: 19). His characteristic expression is *that it might be fulfilled which was spoken of the Lord by the prophet,* occurring thirteen times. Matthew gives us sixty quotations from the Old Testament. It is logical that Matthew should stand first among the twenty-seven books of the New Testament.

The Gospel relates the life of Jesus Christ from His birth to the giving of the Great Commission in Galilee. Matthew's opening verse is a door which swings backward into the Old Testament and also forward into the New Testament: *The book of the generation of*

Jesus Christ, the son of David, the son of Abraham."

When Matthew left his job of tax collection, he brought with him more than pen and ink. He brought the ability to classify and codify parables, miracles, sermons and teachings through which runs a common thought; for his biography of Christ is written topically rather than chronologically.

In developing his great theme of the Kingship of Christ, Matthew first writes of the person of the King (1:1-4: 16), then of the program of the King and His Kingdom (4: 17-16:20), and finally of the rejection of the King, His crucifixion under the title *"This is Jesus of Nazareth, the King of the Jews,"* and the resurrection (16:21 - 28:20).

Matthew alone records the visit of the Magi who came seeking the King of the Jews. He shows in Jesus' life the fulfillment of Isaiah's prophecy of the Virgin Birth and incarnation (Isa. 7: 14); of Micah's prophecy of Bethlehem as the birthplace of the Lord; of Jeremiah's prophecy of the slaughter of the innocents; of Isaiah's prophecy of the ministry of the forerunner, John the Baptist; and so on through Christ's life to the very end in the betrayal, death and resurrection. Matthew matches the Old Testament prophecies with their complete fulfillment in the One whom he seeks to prove is the King of the Jews.

The essence of Matthew is given in both the message of Jesus Christ and of John the Baptist, His forerunner: *"Repent ye: for the kingdom of heaven is at hand."* Matthew repeats the phrase, "the kingdom of heaven," thirty-three times in this connection.

The theme of Kingship which characterizes all that Matthew wrote of Jesus led the early church fathers to adopt the lion as the symbol to represent Matthew's Gospel in the art of the early church. The theme is sustained to the very final note in the triumphant risen King's own claim of universal dominion on which claim he commanded. His great disciples were commanded to evangelize all nations to His standard. *"All power is given unto me in heaven and in earth. Go ye therefore, and teach all nations ..."* (28:18,19).

MARK

~

The Story of Jesus Christ as the Servant of God

Although the Gospel of Mark is anonymous, there is adequate reason to ascribe the authorship of the book with certainty to John Mark, the attendant of Peter and a companion and servant of the Apostle Paul. Mark wrote the story after the death of these apostles, as he had often heard it from their lips.

He wrote in Rome, and his use of Latin terms in explanation of Jewish words and customs indicate that his writing was directed to the Roman mind. His purpose seems to be primarily evangelistic. Several striking peculiarities of Mark's account make it unique among the other accounts. The manner of writing has been described as graphic, forceful, and dramatic. He does not often refer to the Old Testament prophecies as Matthew does, because the Romans knew little of those prophecies. For the same reason he gave no genealogy of Christ as Matthew and Luke did to whom they wrote.

To the Romans the great things of life were action, service, and efficiency. Mark seizes this as his opportunity to picture Jesus Christ to them appealingly as the mighty wonder-working servant of God. His key expressions are *"straightway," "immediately," "forthwith."* Words of unusual forcefulness are used with dramatic and graphic effect. His keynote is found in chapter 10:44, 45: *"Whosoever of you will be the chiefest, shall be servant of all. For even the Son of man came not to be ministered unto, but to minister, and to give his life a ransom for many."*

As befits the story of a servant, Mark is

characteristically a Gospel of deeds rather than of discourses. He has room for twenty miracles and references to many more, but he finds room for only four parables.

Jesus and His disciples are constantly at work. If He seeks rest from the work by retirement to the desert, His purpose is defeated by the people for whom He performed miracles, or if His rest should be sleeping during the storm at sea, His disciples ask Him to perform to them the mighty work of stilling the tempest. Thus, disease, demons, darkness of the soul and depths of the sea are wrought upon by this ministering servant of God, for the benefit of man and the glory of God.

Mark even removed the offense of the cross from the Roman mind by showing it as the culmination of all His service to humanity, and reminding them that the Roman centurion in charge of the crucifixion under the cross went away from the cross saying, *"Truly this man was the Son of God."*

The early Christians used the ox as the symbol to represent Mark's Gospel in the art of the early church because the ox represents both service and sacrifice (Mark's key passage makes this clear), as the lion represented the Kingship of Christ as set forth by Matthew.

With Mark, Christ's working did not cease even with the completion of the work of redemption, for He was *"received up into heaven, and sat on the right hand of God. And they (His disciples) went forth, and preached everywhere, the Lord working with them. . ."* (16:19,20).

LUKE

~

The Story of
Jesus Christ as the
Son of Man

The author of the Gospel of Luke and the Book of Acts is mentioned in three passages (Col 4:14; Phil. 24; 2 Tim 4:11). We learn from these verses that Luke, or Lucas, was a physician and a fellow worker of St Paul. He accompanied Paul in his first imprisonment in Rome and was the Apostle's sole companion during the second and final imprisonment.

As he had learned it in his companionship with Paul, the great Apostle and missionary to the Gentiles, Luke, a Greek scholar, wrote the story of Jesus to confirm it in the minds of his Greek friend, Theophilus, who had already believed the truth of the Gospel. Some have thought that Luke's secondary purpose was to demonstrate that Christianity was not politically dangerous. These purposes are revealed when the writer parallels Gospel events with contemporary history (1:5; 2:1, 2; 3:1, 2).

Luke began his account with a classical prologue. He was skillful in the Greek and had a versatile vocabulary. The great "hobby" of the Greek was perfect manhood, and Luke, finding the perfection of manhood in Christ, wrote to them to commend Him to them as the *"ideal man,"* the Son of Man, the Saviour and perfecter of mankind.

The key passage of the book is recorded in chapter 19, verse 10: *"For the Son of man is come to seek and to save that which was lost."* Luke views Jesus as the Saviour of every race, of Gentiles and Samaritans as well as Jews: a Saviour whose special interest seems to be in the poor and the outcast, the women and children, and the prodigal sons of all ages.

His is the universal Gospel; as such his genealogy of Christ traced back to Adam to show that he belongs to humanity, whereas Matthew stops his genealogy with Abraham to show that Christ belongs to the Jewish race.

Luke's account of the birth of Christ was from the standpoint of Mary. Matthew's account was from the standpoint of Joseph. Luke's account is unique for he recorded the birth of John the Baptist, and he alone recorded the birth and childhood of Christ, the presentation in the temple, and the visit to the temple at the age of twelve. The story of the encounter with Zacchaeus, the mocking of Christ by Herod, are also told. These and many similar incidents have brought Luke the distinction of writing the Gospel of womanhood and childhood.

In championing the cause of the poor and the outcast, Luke alone records the parable of the rich man and Lazarus, the rich fool, the prodigal son, the Pharisee and the Publican, and the Good Samaritan. These events which the other Evangelists missed, as well as those which Luke records in common with the others, show the trend and purpose of Luke's story. He paints Jesus Christ as the ideal man who belongs to humanity as its brother and Saviour. Christ is the perfect man who has come to perfect sinners through His shed blood, even for the outcast and the publican. Had Luke recorded nothing more than that most beautiful of all stories, the prodigal son, he would have

His Gospel of hope.

The early Christians caught this spirit and purpose of Luke's Gospel and made *"the face of man"*, the symbol to represent Luke in the art of the church, as the lion and the ox represent Matthew and Mark.

In the first chapter of his book, Luke recorded five Christian hymns, and the rest of his story of the Son of man, Jesus Christ, who has put a song into the hearts of innumerable thousands of the poor, the publican, and the prodigal, who otherwise would not have been able to find in their hearts or hopes anything to inspire a song.

The effect of this Gospel is precisely that which is expressed in the purpose stated by Luke. The narrative is so real and well expressed that it makes us see Jesus as an actual figure of history. Luke 19: 10: *"For the son of man came to seek and to save that which was lost,"* is amply illustrated by Luke's Gospel. The concluding words of the Gospel connect the historical reality with doctrinal truth and show that the revelation through Christ is the basis for the preaching of repentance and of forgiveness of sins.

JOHN

~

The Story of
Jesus Christ as the
Son of God

The Gospel of John is regarded by many as the most profound book in the New Testament. Simple in language and structure, it is nevertheless a deeply perceptive exposition of the person and the spiritual teaching of the Lord Jesus Christ in a historical setting and carries us to the loftiest heights of revealed truth.

John, the beloved disciple of Christ, was one of the sons of Zebedee (Mark 1:19, 20), a fisherman of Galilee, and of Salome, who was probably the sister of Mary, the mother of Jesus (Matt. 27:56; Mark 15:40; John 19:25). The episodes of Jesus' life in which John shared are too many to list. He was thus qualified to paint a picture of Jesus Christ as no other person could.

Like the synoptic Gospel, the Gospel of John has as its theme the presentation of Christ to His own people (nation). Thus, John presents the work of John the Baptist, the gathering of His disciples, the teaching of the people, the performing of miracles to illustrate different areas of His power, the stirring of opposition on the part of the religious leaders of Israel, and His condemnation to death by the Council. The latter was implemented by Pilate the Roman governor, leading to His crucifixion and resurrection (with appearances to His chosen disciples).

The keynote to the Gospel is the author's own statement in chapter 20: 30, 31: *"And many other signs truly did Jesus in the presence of his disciples, which are not written in this book; But these are written, that ye might believe that Jesus is the Christ, the Son of God; and that believing ye might have life through his name."* Prominent in this brief passage are the words: signs, believe, and life. They provide logical organization for the Gospel. In the *"signs"* is the revelation of God; in *"belief"* is the reaction that they are designed to produce; in *"life"* is the result which belief brings.

True to his aim, John traces Christ's genealogy not from Abraham, as Matthew did, nor back to Adam as Luke did, but back to God in eternity. *"In the beginning was the Word, and the Word was with God, and the Word was God"* (1:1). So the Gospel of John is the Gospel of Christ's deity, as that of Luke is the Gospel of His humanity, Mark of His servanthood, and Matthew of His Kingship. John tells of the mystery of the incarnation of the deity in humanity in simple words, *"the Word was made flesh, and dwelt among us, (and we beheld his glory, the glory as of the only begotten of the Father,) full of grace and truth"* (1:14). To prove his case, John points us to these witnesses concerning Christ: God the Father, Christ Himself, and His miracles, John the Baptist, the Old Testament Scriptures, and the Holy Spirit.

He recorded seven great *"signs"* or miracles wrought by Christ before His crucifixion of which only one was mentioned by the synoptics (2: 1-11; 4:46-54; 5:1-9; 6:1-14; 6:16-21; 9:1-12; 11:1-46). He also recorded seven great claims of Christ, most of which are closely associated with the miracles which served as proofs of His right to make such claims as no one but God could presume to make: *"I am the bread of life"* (6: 35), *"I am the light of the world"* (8:12; 9:5), *"I am the door"* (10:7), *"I am the good shepherd"* (10: 11, 14), *"I* am the resurrection and the life" (11:25), "I am the way, the truth, and the life" (14:6), and "I am the true vine" (15: 1).

John's plan in his Gospel is truly beautiful. His arrangement is superb. We see the Word, i.e., Christ, in His pre-incarnate glory, so that we may appreciate His condescending love in coming to earth to save sinners. In His early ministry He reveals Himself to ever-widening circles, but was rejected in both Judaea and Galilee. Nevertheless, Christ does not at once destroy those who have rejected Him, but instead makes His tender appeal to sinners to repent and to accept Him by faith.

By two mighty deeds, He now manifests Himself clearly as the Messiah. But though the Greeks seek Him, the Jews, who have seen clear tokens of His character, love, compassion, and power, repulse Him. So, He turns to the inner circle, tenderly instructing His Disciples in the upper room. In His very death He overcomes Satan and the world, and by means of His victorious resurrection, He reveals the meaning of the cross.

ACTS

~

The First History
of the Church

The Book of Acts could more properly be named *"The Acts of the Ascended Christ"* or *"The Acts of the Holy Spirit Through the Church."* Its seventy-one references to the Holy Spirit almost entitle it to be named "The Gospel of the Holy Spirit." Although this book is called the Acts of the Apostles, it does not narrate the deeds of all the earliest apostles of Christ. The record is more or less selective, and is apparently motivated by a desire to trace the growth of the Church from the day of Pentecost through the expansion to Antioch, and then through the Pauline missions to Rome, Ephesus, Corinth, etc.

The organization of the book is largely biographical, focusing on personalities such as Peter, Stephen, Philip, Barnabas, and Paul. Acts is itself not a unity, for it is obviously designed as a sequel to Luke. The writer speaks of *"the former treatise"* (Acts 1: 1), and his address to Theophilus indicates a relationship to the Gospel which is addressed to the same person.

The summary of that former treatise, (Acts 1:1, 2), accords exactly with the content of Luke and resumes the narrative at the point where Luke dropped it. There can be no reasonable doubt that Acts and Luke are two volumes of one work. Both were designed to fulfill the same purpose of confirming personal faith and of providing an understandable historical record of God's revelation to men in the work of Christ, through His personal career and through His church.

Chapter one, verse eight, gives us not only the keynote of the entire book, but indicates its plan and outline as well: *"But ye shall receive power, after that the Holy Ghost is come upon you: and ye shall be witnesses unto me both in Jerusalem, and in all Judea, and in Samaria, and unto the uttermost part of the earth."* Chapters one and two record the reception of the promised power on the day of Pentecost; the witness in Jerusalem as recorded in chapters 3:1 to 6:7; the witness in Judaea in 6:8 to 8:3; the witness in Samaria in 8:4 to 8:40; and the witness to *"the uttermost part of the earth"* in 9 to 28.

In the Petrine section of the book, the church is seen growing under the guidance of the Holy Spirit from a pronouncedly Jewish sect into a broad cosmopolitan body where all racial distinctions between Jews and Gentiles are obliterated. This trend continues in the Pauline section, wherein the church became predominantly Gentile in its spirit and membership through the fiery zeal and ceaseless activity of Paul, the great missionary and Apostle to the Gentiles, whose three missionary journeys are recorded.

The Book of Acts records how the conviction of the resurrection of the Lord Jesus Christ and the coming of the Holy Spirit transformed Peter, the cowardly denier, into the courageous Pentecost preacher, and Saul the chief persecutor of the church into its chief apostle and missionary.

As these Spirit-filled witnesses disseminated the gospel, the church expanded from Jerusalem, its birthplace; to Samaria to break down an ancient prejudice; and on to Ephesus to purify it of the vulgarities of

Diana. From Ephesus it was to go into Europe to Athens and Corinth to supplant Greek culture with the nobler culture of the Christian ethic, and to Rome which was then the center of world power. Thus was Jesus' command fulfilled. And *"the Lord added to the church daily such as should be saved,"* not only individuals but countries, until his enemies charged His disciples that they had *"turned the world upside down."*

All was done in the midst of terrific persecution from both Jews and Gentiles. Yes, "the blood of the martyrs became the seed of the church," verifying the promise of the Head of the church that *"the gates of hell shall not prevail against it."*

ROMANS

~

The Way of Salvation
in Six Great Words

The Epistle to the Romans, which Samuel Coleridge calls *"the profoundest book in existence,"* was written by the Apostle Paul from Corinth as a substitute for immediate personal contact and as preparatory to making the Roman church a missionary center comparable to Antioch, Ephesus, Philippi, and other cities.

Undoubtedly, it is Paul's masterpiece, a textbook of all the Epistles in the New Testament. The theme of the book is the revelation of the righteousness of God to man, and its application to his spiritual need or the way of salvation. Its theme is thus the basis of all Christian experience, because man cannot do business with God until a proper approach has been established.

This epistle is directed mainly to Gentiles, Paul himself being a missionary to the Gentiles (1:5). He sketched the religious history of the Gentile world as the prelude (1:18-32); he asserted that God's salvation is for Jews and Gentiles (3:29) — that there is no "distinction" between Jews and Gentiles in the faith. Romans avers that salvation is universal in scope.

The key passage is in chapter 1:16, 17, *"For I am not ashamed of the gospel of Christ: for it is the power of God unto salvation to every one that believeth; to the Jew first, and also to the Greek. For therein is the righteousness of God revealed from faith to faith: as it is written, The just shall live by faith."* From this basic statement Paul evolves the profound argument of the epistle which may be summarized in six great words;

namely, condemnation, justification, sanctification, glorification, restoration, and consecration.

"Condemnation" is what all men deserve because of their unrighteousness and sin as the result of the fall of Adam, the father of all men. The wrath of God was incurred by all men through the fall of Adam. Thus the mouth of every man may be stopped, and all the world become guilty before God. This is the argument of chapters 1-3:20.

"Justification" is the way by which condemnation is removed and the righteousness of God is imputed to (charged to the account of) the unrighteous through faith in the shed blood of Jesus Christ, without any deed of the Law whatsoever. *"As by the offense of one judgment came upon all men to condemnation; even so by the righteousness of one the free gift came upon all men unto justification of life"* (5: 18). This is the argument of chapters 3:20-5:21.

"Sanctification," and not a license to sin for grace to abound, will be the result of the abounding grace of justification. *"Shall we continue in sin, that grace may abound? God forbid."* Rather the justified believer walks not after the flesh and the world, but after the Spirit, and through the Spirit the deeds of the body are mortified. This process of sanctification is dealt with in chapters 6:1-8:13.

"Glorification" is the goal of justification and sanctification. Our glory is that we are the children of God, and *"joint heirs with Christ"*; for *"whom he justified, them he also glorified.* "This argument proceeds in chapter 8:14-39.

"**Restoration**" is the word Paul used to sum up the argument he makes in chapter 9 to 11 for the solution to the *"Jewish question."* God hath not cast away his ancient chosen people of Israel, but because of their unbelief they were broken off. *"They also, if they abide not still in unbelief, shall be grafted in: for God is able to graft them in again,"* i.e., Israel will be restored. (We have also been restored to the place Adam lost in the Garden of Eden.)

"**Consecration**" is the great practical word which sums up the last five chapters and to which all the doctrinal words of the first eleven chapters lead. It shows the manner in which doctrine is made the motive power of practice. *"I beseech you therefore, brethren, by the mercies of God, that ye present your bodies a living sacrifice, holy, acceptable unto God, which is your reasonable service"* (12:1).

Thus it is with Paul's great epistles: first comes **doctrine,** then follows **practice,** and between these, like a golden hinge, a *"therefore,"* showing that "**doctrine**" is the root, or foundation, and that "**practice**" is the fruit of Christianity. Let no man (Christians), therefore, despise doctrine, for it is the foundation of eternal life, and let not those who confess the Christian doctrine fail to translate it into consecrated Christian living.

FIRST CORINTHIANS

~

Faults Corrected

In the course of his European mission, the second missionary journey, Paul came to Corinth from Athens and began his labors in the synagogue. After Paul's departure at the end of 18 months' ministry, Apollos came and ministered, for a time (Acts 18:24, 27-28). The church seems to have been composed mainly of Gentiles, for the testimony in the synagogue was soon terminated by the opposition of the Jews (Acts 18:6, 7).

Paul made contact with the church after his departure. Knowledge of its conditions reached him through the household of Chloe (1:11), and a letter sent to him by the congregation. Paul had written an earlier epistle, probably brief and limited in its scope, which has not been preserved.

In their letter to Paul, his advice was asked on a number of questions of vital importance. Apparently, the church of Corinth caused the Apostle more concern than any other that he founded, as his letters to this congregation seem to demonstrate. Despite the necessity for correction and warning, Paul does not fail to mingle his assurance of love and concern.

In answer to their questions and to correct certain faults of the church of which Paul had heard, he wrote this letter. The first four chapters of the epistle deal with the party spirit which had divided the Corinthian Christians into rival factions bearing the names of Paul, Apollos, Peter, and Christ. Paul's remedy for this fault both then and now was that all human teachers of the Gospel should be submerged and lost in Christ, the Head of the church, and to realize that they are ministers of Christ, and stewards of the mysteries of God

Chapters 5 and 6 correct the existing immorality which was unrebuked in the church, and also the fault of church members going to law before heathen tribunals to settle their differences. Chapter 7 answers the questions they had asked about marriage relations: its advantages and disadvantages, its usefulness and abuse in the immoral surrounding of the Corinthians of that day.

Chapters 8 to 10 proclaim in a masterly manner the interrelation of the fundamental social principles of true liberty and love for the guidance of the Christian's conduct in *things questionable.* *"Personal liberty"* is not to be allowed to place a stumbling block in the way of the weaker brother. The law of love is thus supreme even over liberty. *"If meat make my brother to offend, I will eat no flesh while the world standeth, lest I make my brother to offend.*" Paul's rule for the determination of a Christian's duty in "things questionable" is still unexcelled, namely, *"whatsoever you do, do all to the glory of God."*

Chapters 11 to 14 correct the abuse of the Lord's Supper and the misuse of spiritual gifts and the rivalry between those possessing different gifts. The controlling principle is ever to be love, the first fruit of the Spirit on which Paul writes a classic in the thirteenth chapter which is unexcelled in all literature. *"Love never faileth"* truly is the greatest virtue in the world.

Chapter 15 is the greatest resurrection chapter in the Bible with its grand doxology of victory for the Christian over sin, death, and the grave. *"O death: where is thy sting? O grave, where is thy victory? The sting of death is sin; and the strength of sin is the law. But thanks be to God, which giveth us the victory through our Lord Jesus Christ"* (15:55-57). This is the climax of the doctrine of the epistle, which Paul immediately connects to practice. *"Therefore, my beloved brethren, be ye steadfast, unmoveable, always abounding in the work of the Lord, forasmuch as ye know that your labor is not in vain in the Lord"* (15:58).

SECOND CORINTHIANS

~

Paul's Defense of His Ministry

Paul's first letter to the Corinthians had the desired effect of correcting the moral and spiritual faults at which he aimed. But the opposition to Paul which was fostered by various factions was centered in his apostleship and authority. It was fanned by the arrival in Corinth of men who claimed to belong to the Christian fellowship and to be of the same apostolic rank (2 Cor. 11:13).

It seems that the apostle felt necessary to leave his work at Ephesus temporarily to make a hurried trip to Corinth to settle the unrest (2: 1). Even this face-to-face encounter was not successful. On his return to Ephesus, Paul wrote an epistle with tears and anguish (2:4; 7:8), and sent it by the hand of Titus. Anxiety over the outcome compounded his troubled situation at Ephesus, where he faced the danger of death (1:8). Finally Paul, after leaving Ephesus, passed through Troas (2:12, 13) where he met Titus in Macedonia and learned with relief the improvement of conditions in the Corinthian church. This news led to the writing of 2 Corinthians, in which Paul defends and expounds his ministry (2:14-7:4).

Paul informs the Corinthians in this Epistle of the comfort their repentance had brought to him. But his enemies at Corinth sought to turn the Christians against him for writing the first Epistle instead of his coming to them in person. They ridiculed his appearance and mannerisms, disparaged his apostleship and questioned his authority and sincerity.

Paul's reply to these criticisms makes this letter the

most severe of all his letters with the exception of his letter to the Galatians. Surely no other of his letters is so full of heart throbs as is this one.

The keynote to the letter is recorded in chapter 4:5. *"For we preach not ourselves, but Christ Jesus the Lord; and ourselves your servants for Jesus' sake."* In the first seven chapters Paul gives a defense of his ministry. It had been a triumphant ministry, the Corinthians themselves in their changed manner of life being his letter of commendation. His was a ministry whose only motives were the fear of God and the constraining love of Christ. It was an unselfish ministry, for them and not for what they had, maintaining himself by his trade as a tent-maker, *"Giving no offense in anything, that the ministry be not blamed."*

In chapters 8 and 9 Paul dealt with the offering being gathered throughout the churches for the relief of the poor Christians in Jerusalem. To inspire the Corinthians with the true spirit of liberality, he cited the example of the liberality of the Macedonians, relating how in *"a great trial of affliction the abundance of their joy and their deep poverty abounded unto the riches of their liberality,"* because they *"first gave their own selves to the Lord."*

He tapped the foundation of true charity by saying, *"Ye know the grace of our Lord Jesus Christ, that, though he was rich, yet for your sakes he became poor, that ye through his poverty might be rich."* He closes the subject with a shout , *"Thanks be unto God for his unspeakable gift."* The giver who remembers Calvary wilt eventually give not only liberally but "hilariously."

In the last four chapters, Paul came back to the subject of his ministry to vindicate his apostleship, which his enemies had questioned. His bodily presence might be weak, but Paul was commended by Christ Himself in most marvelous visions and revelation granted to him, as well as by the manifest way in which Christ had attended him in all his persecution, perils and imprisonment. Christ had honored Paul's ministry in the extension of the church in such a way as to place him not one whit behind the very chiefest apostle.

Though this letter is most severe in parts, it closes with the richest of the Scriptural benedictions, *"The grace of the Lord Jesus Christ, and the love of God, and the communion of the Holy Ghost, be with you all. "*

GALATIANS

~

Law and Grace

This work of Paul is significant for many reasons. Interpretationally, there is here a great contribution to the understanding of the Gospel and its practical implications. Historically, it saved Christianity from becoming a sect of Judaism in Paul's day. It also fanned the fires of the 16th Century Reformation which saved Christianity from Romanism.

Doctrinally, it argues that since justification is by faith alone, so faith is the only proper sphere of Christian living. Galatians is also called the great **"Magna Charta of Christian Liberty."** Here Paul champions the cause of spiritual liberty in Christ for those who were once emancipated by the Gospel he had preached and very shortly afterward were brought again into bondage by certain Judaizing teachers.

The Epistle to the Galatians is the forerunner and the epitome of the letter to the Romans. The theme stated briefly in Galatians and expanded in Romans is justification by faith alone without the deeds of the law. Paul's purpose, then, is not to prove primarily that justification is by faith. His argument assumes this is true, and so builds upon the fact that justification has granted them perfect standing with God and full inheritance with Abraham. He seeks to establish that sanctification is in faith apart from adherence to any part of Mosaic Law. This is the contention of the whole letter.

The key that unlocks the book is found in chapter 2:16, *"Knowing that a man is not justified by the works of the law, but by the faith of Jesus Christ, even we have believed in Jesus Christ, that we might be justified by the faith of Christ, and not by the works of the law: for by the works of the law shall no flesh be justified."*

Paul marvels at the fickleness of the Galatians for having been swept away from the true Gospel he had preached, to another. Gospel (1:18), which was really no Gospel at all, he cries, *"O foolish Galatians, who hath bewitched you?"*

The false teachers who had undone so much of Paul's work made it necessary for him to defend his apostleship by showing that it had been received directly from Christ and had been recognized by the other apostles as on a par with their own. Such defensive subjects make up the first two chapters. In chapters 3 and 4, Paul assumes the offensive and carries the war into the enemy's territory by proclaiming the doctrine of grace and liberty of the Gospel contrasted with the restrictions and bondage of the Mosaic Law.

The law was temporary and never intended to save; it was the scaffolding, not the permanent building. When the child reaches his maturity, the guardian loses his position. So Paul reasons that the *"law was our schoolmaster to bring us unto Christ, that we might be justified by faith. But after that faith is come, we are no longer under a schoolmaster."* After the concrete is "set," the form which gave it shape is removed.

"Christ hath redeemed us from the curse of the law, being made a curse for us." This is a real "Emancipation Proclamation" for every Christian. The last two

chapters are an exhortation to make practical use in life of the liberty proclaimed, *"Stand fast therefore in the liberty wherewith Christ hath made us free, and be not entangled again with the yoke of bondage."* The new life is not legalism or license but liberty disciplined by grace and directed by the Spirit of God in love. Christians are to walk in the Spirit and not to fulfill the lust of the flesh; rather they are to crucify the flesh with its affections and lust.

To illustrate how this must be done, St. Paul shows them the three crosses of the Christian's perpetual calvary with the Cross of Christ central and about it on either side a cross for the world of sin and one for itself: *"God forbid that I should glory, (or boast) save in the cross of our Lord Jesus Christ, by whom the world is crucified unto me, and I unto the world."*

EPHESIANS

~

The Church Letter

The ministry of Paul in Ephesus was singularly effective. For more than two years (Acts 19:8, 10), he was able to preach unhindered, first in the synagogue and later in the school of Tyrannus (Acts 19:9). He performed special miracles and reached the populace of Ephesus and of the province as a whole more thoroughly than he did the people of any other place. Luke said that *"all they which dwelt in Asia heard the Word of the Lord Jesus, both Jews and Greeks"* (Acts 19: 10), *"So mightily grew the word of God and prevailed"* (Acts 19:20), and that so many had believed that idolatry suffered great economic loss (Acts 19:26,27). The Church at Ephesus became a missionary center and for centuries was one of the strongholds of Christianity in Asia Minor.

At Ephesus was located the great temple of Diana, which was one of the seven wonders of the ancient world. The epistle gives evidence of having been written during a prison experience (3:1; 4:1). There is reason to believe that it was composed at Rome shortly after his letter to the Colossians and sent along with that Epistle and the one to Philemon by the hand of Tychicus (Eph. 6:21, 22; Col. 4:7, 8), to inform the Ephesians that in the Christian church they have a temple infinitely glorious.

Ephesians is pre-eminently the church epistle. If the critics of the church knew this letter better, they would criticize less, and if Christians knew it better, there would be no room for criticism.

The key word in Ephesians is *"mystery,"* the first

occurring in 1:9, 10. Here Paul identifies the controlling theme of the epistle, namely, the design of God's overall plan. God's purposes and ultimate union of all things in Christ, and the main instrument which He is using during the present age to accomplish this goal, is the church.

The first three chapters are doctrinal, and deal with the divine creation of the church. The last three chapters are practical, and deal with the human conduct of the church. In chapter one Paul shows the "blue-prints" of the church drawn in heaven in the eternities "before the foundation of the world." According to the Divine Architect's plan, Jesus Christ was given to be the head over all things, the church, His body, the fullness of Him that filleth all in all.

In chapter two, he shows the construction of the church in accordance with this eternal plan. The marvel of it all is that this glorious temple is built entirely of waste material, which was once *"dead in trespasses and sins,"* given over to *"the lust of the flesh"* and *"by nature the children of wrath."* This material, whether of Jewish or Gentile extraction, is welded into one body of the cross of Jesus Christ, and "built upon the foundation of the apostles and prophets, Jesus Christ himself being the chief cornerstone; in whom all the building fitly framed together groweth unto an holy temple in the Lord."

In chapter three, Paul goes on to point out the glorious ministry of the church: *"To the intent that now unto the principalities and powers in heavenly places might* be known by the church the manifold wisdom of God." To throw light outward to enlighten men would be glory enough, but to the church is given the further glory of throwing this light upward to enlighten angels in the heavenly places as to what grace can do for sinners.

Then let those in the seat of the scornful mock and belittle the church! Her glory still abides as the spiritual temple of God and the body of Christ, of which He is both the head and the chief cornerstone. Paul begins the practical part of the epistle by enjoining the Ephesians to preserve the unity of the church because there is "one Lord, one faith, one baptism, one God and Father of all."

The Ephesian Christians are to put off the old man in the regenerate life. They are to be imitators of God as dear children and are to walk as children of light. Thus Paul outlines the life to be lived by wives, husbands, children, servants, and all who make up this glorious church.

To do this will require conflict, for which God provided a sufficient armor in the girdle of truth, the breastplate of righteousness, the sandals of the gospel, the shield of faith, the helmet of salvation and the sword of the Spirit, which is the Word of God. Equipped with this whole armor of God, the Christian will "be able to withstand in the evil day, and having done all, to stand."

PHILIPPIANS

~

Paul's "Joy Letter"

Philippians is a hortatory letter written by St. Paul and addressed to the church at Philippi. Together with Colossians, Philemon and Ephesians, all form the fourfold cluster of the Prison Epistles written from Rome.

This letter engages in no harsh censure, although Paul lovingly reproaches Euodia and Syntyche for their lack of harmony (4:2). This apparently was a root cause of disunity in the church, necessitating Paul's call to agreement (1:27; 2:1-4,14). With many references to individuals it is certainly one of his most personal letters. It is also regarded as an inspired thank you letter for the gift which the church has sent to Paul (4:10-20), as well as an epistle of commendation for his fellow workers, Timothy and Epaphroditus.

Philippians is pre-eminently the love letter of all Paul's epistles, full of tenderness and expression of affection. The church at Philippi was the first Christian church in Europe, established by Paul during his second missionary journey.

The Philippians had not forgotten their debt of gratitude to Paul. Regularly they sent gifts to sustain him in his work, and now that he was a prisoner of Nero at Rome, they sent Epaphroditus with an offering to relieve his prison hardships. Later they were distressed to learn that their messenger had taken sick in Rome, and was at the point of death. Paul, hearing of their anxiety, wrote this epistle to thank them for their gift and the love it expressed.

The predominant note of the letter is joy, rejoicing, gladness. These and kindred expressions occur twenty-four times. It was at Philippi ten years earlier that Paul and Silas, with their backs still bleeding from their scourging, sang in their dungeons at midnight, and this letter is another such a "song in the night," for it is also a joy song from a prison cell. It is a case of one who was *"sorrowful, yet always rejoicing, as poor, yet making many rich; as having nothing, and yet possessing all things."*

Paul tells us the secret of this unconquerable joy in chapter 1:21, which is the key verse of the epistle. *"For to me to live is Christ, and to die is gain."* If his imprisonment enables him to witness better for Christ, then nothing could bring him more joy than imprisonment for Christ's sake. He never thinks of himself as Nero's prisoner but as the *"prisoner of Jesus Christ."* If death brings him home to be with the Lord, then death will be welcomed with joy though it come by way of Nero's sword. If the lack of all things on his part brings glory to Christ, then Paul will rejoice in his poverty and hardships.

True joy is to be found not in things but in Christ. Therefore, Paul says, *"Rejoice in the Lord always, and again I say, Rejoice."* Do we want to be able to rejoice always, regardless of our outward circumstances? Do we covet the spirit of contentment with our lot, even though it may be the bondage of sickness, poverty or persecution? Paul points the way by saying, *"Let this mind be in you, which was also in Christ Jesus: Who, being in the form of God, thought it not robbery to be equal with*

God. But made himself of no reputation, and took upon him the form of a servant, and was made in the likeness of men: And being found in fashion as a man, he humbled himself, and became obedient unto death, even the death of the cross" (2:5-8).

This is the mind of Christ, a mind of serving, loving and self-sacrifice, and it is the only way that leads to true contentment and abiding joy. Having this mind of Christ, Paul would say: *"I have learned, in whatsoever state I am, therewith to be content."*

Christianity and "a long face" do not belong together. But Christianity and joy are inseparable mates, and Paul's message to the Philippian Christians and Christians of every age (the bride of Christ), concerning these two is *"what therefore God hath joined together, let not man put asunder."*

COLOSSIANS

~

Christ Pre-eminent

This Epistle is almost universally regarded as a genuine writing of St. Paul. Three times the writer calls himself Paul (1:1; 1:23; 4:18). Colossians and Ephesians are twin epistles. Their resemblance is so great that those who have doubted Paul's authorship of Ephesians have averred that it is only a copy of Colossians with additions. The great concepts of the person and work of Christ, death and resurrection with Christ, harmonious domestic relationships, and the new man in Christ are unmistakably Pauline.

The occasion of writing to the Colossians was the projected mission of Tychicus, coupled with a report brought to Paul from Colosse by Epaphras (1:7-9; 4: 12). Apparently, this report informed Paul of insidious errors, both doctrinal and practical, that had crept into the church. The Colossian heresy, as it is often called, combined Judaistic elements with ascetic and gnostic teachings akin to those features which later developed into a full-blown gnostic system, a man-made religion.

Paul had neither founded nor visited the church at Colosse, but he heard from them through Epaphras and wrote commending them for their faith and to warn them of dangers from false teaching that beset them. There were those at Colosse, as among the Galatians, who sought to enslave the Colossians with legalistic observances of Sabbaths and New Moons and other ritualism. Other false teachers advocated the worship of angels. Still others who saw evil in all matters, denied the creatorship of God and the deity of Christ, and they practiced a slavish asceticism.

The basic purpose of the book of Colossians is to combat these heresies by proclaiming Christ's deity and pre-eminence in all things. The key passage of the epistle is found in chapter 2:9, 10, *"For in him (Christ) dwelleth all the fullness of the Godhead bodily, and ye are complete in him, which is the head of all principality and power."*

Sometimes it is difficult to see how in Paul's day and ours there could be denial of the deity of Christ even in the church, in the face of such positive statements as Paul makes to the Colossians that Christ is *"the image of the invisible God, the firstborn of every creature: For by him were all things created, that are in heaven, and that are in the earth, visible and invisible."* Paul's passion for Christ was that the Colossians *"Crown Him Lord of all,"* for he says, *"He is the head of the body, the church: who is the beginning, the first born from the dead; that in all things he might have the preeminence. For it pleased the Father that in him should all fullness dwell. "*

Thus Paul sets forth the doctrine of the deity, sufficiency, and pre-eminence of Christ in the first part of the letter. Then, as in the other epistles, he turns to the doctrinal and practical being connected by his customary *"therefore,"* like a golden hinge between the two: *"Mortify, therefore, your members which are upon the earth." "Put on the new man. . . . Put on... bowels of mercies, kindness. . . . And above all these things put on love, which is the bond of perfectness."* Thus, in the most practical manner Paul shows the Colossians how to live the Christian life, giving Christ pre-eminence in all things regardless of their situation in life, whether

it be that of a husband or wife, parent or child, master
or servant.

FIRST & SECOND THESSALONIANS

~

The Second Coming of Christ

These Epistles are among the first of Paul's writings. They testify of the fact that the message which Paul preached was not novelty, but that it had been a settled faith for some time.

The First Epistle to the Thessalonians is the earliest of the New Testament books. It was written about 52 A.D. or early in the year 53 A.D., a few months after Paul was driven from Thessalonica to Berea (Acts 17:11), as a result of the intense opposition which attended the establishment of the church there. The persecution continued to harass the little band of believers whom Paul had won from Gentile idolatry at Thessalonica. In spite of the persecution, the church flourished as Paul's correspondence shows. He sent Timothy to encourage the church and to prepare a report as to how they were standing the test (1 Thess. 3:1-5).

The first letter was written upon the receipt of the report that Timothy brought back to Corinth, and it included his name and that of Silas in its greeting. Its content is twofold: praise for their steadfastness under persecution by the Jews and the correction of certain errors and misunderstanding that had grown up among them. The main doctrinal theme of both First and Second Thessalonians is the second advent of Christ, a topic scarcely mentioned in Galatians unless it appears in Paul's allusion to waiting for the hope of righteousness (Gal. 5:5). This doctrine is the hope which Paul held up to sustain the Thessalonians under persecution.

He commends them for the way they have *"turned*

to God from idols to serve the living and true God; And to wait for his Son from heaven." Paul asks what is his hope, or joy, or crown of rejoicing, and answers, that it is themselves, *"in the presence of our Lord Jesus Christ at his coming."* His prayer was that they might be established *"unblameable in holiness before God at the coming of the Lord Jesus Christ with all his saints."*

But the Thessalonians were worried lest their loved ones who had died would not share in the joy and the glory of Christ's coming. So Paul wrote to comfort them *"concerning them which are asleep,"* and to assure them that those who were alive at the coming of Christ would have no advantage over the dead Christians, for at the coming of the Lord, "the dead in Christ shall rise first: *"Then we which are alive and remain shall be caught up together with them in the clouds, to meet the Lord in the air; and so shall we ever be with the Lord. Wherefore comfort one another with these words"* (1 Thess. 4:16-18). This is the key verse, and represents the basic purpose of the First Epistle to the Thessalonians.

The Second Epistle to the Thessalonians was written a few months after the first one to correct the misunderstanding that *"the day of the Lord is at hand"* (2 Thess.2:2). Perhaps the vehemence with which Paul preached the doctrine had led to a misunderstanding of his preaching or of the allusions contained in the first letter or perhaps, they had received some teaching from a spurious source, for he urged them not to be *"soon shaken in mind... neither by spirit, nor by word, nor letter as from us"* (2:2), (italic author's), which may mean that he was repudiating some teaching falsely attributed to him by others.

The false teachers were doing just what those of our days are doing. They were interpreting the second coming of Christ in the light of calendars and almanacs, instead of in the light of Christ's own words recorded in Matthew 24, Luke 21, and Mark 13. The false teachers had a mania for date setting then, as those with us today. They regarded the day of the Lord as now present, and their persecution as part of the great tribulation which the Lord had foretold would attend His advent.

Thus, Paul undertook to provide them with definite criteria by which they might recognize the approach of *the day of the Lord.* Unfortunately the criteria which were clear to Paul and to the Thessalonians through him are not so easily understandable today. The veiled reference to the "hinderer" (2:6, 7), is difficult of interpretation. Apparently there are three major events which will presage the Lord's coming: (1) a sudden acceleration of apostasy from Godliness (2:3), (2) the removal of some restraining influence (3:6, 7), and (3) the complete unveiling of the incarnation of evil who will be animated by Satan and who will oppose and exalt himself above all that is called God (2:4,9).

Nowhere else in Paul's epistles does this particular aspect of eschatological teaching occur. It was, however, an integral part of Paul's current instruction and was preached by him in the churches.

The exhortation of the third chapter is an

expansion of the charge given in the first epistle to study to be quiet, and to do your own business, and to work with your hands (1 Thess. 4:11). He rebuked the "busy-bodies" who quit working and became a charge to others because they thought Christ was to return immediately to release them from evil and the tensions of the world, and so they were waiting for the appearance of the deliverer. They were out of step with the rest of the church and were depending upon others for their support (2 Thess. 3:6-11). Paul urged them to earn their own living and to mind their own business. He told them that *"if any would not work, neither should he eat."*

The second coming of Christ is still *"that Blessed Hope"* of the church and it should never be allowed to minister either for fear, as though we were not *"Christ's at his coming,"* or to the fanaticism of setting dates. *"Of the times and the seasons, brethren, ye have no need that I should write unto you. For yourselves know perfectly that the day of the Lord so cometh as a thief in the night."* So the Lord Jesus Himself said, *"Occupy till I come."*

FIRST & SECOND
TIMOTHY

~

Advice to Ministers

From the affectionate way in which Paul wrote to Timothy, it would seem that he was Paul's favorite disciple. Timothy had excellent spiritual training under his mother and grandmother, and was well reported of by the brethren (Acts 16:1, 2).

The numerous exhortations and injunctions to Timothy have caused us to believe that he was timid (1 Cor. 16:10, 11) and needed Paul's support. The perilous times of Nero's reign called for exhortations to constancy, especially as Timothy was young and not robust in health (1 Tim. 4:12; 5:23). On the other hand, none of Paul's co-workers was more active than Timothy, and none more trusted and beloved by the apostle (Phil. 2:19-22).

The Epistles to Timothy and Titus are classed as pastoral, because their contents consist of advice regarding the administration of the local church. The Pastoral Epistles as a group are the most valuable source extant for the understanding of the life of the church in the transition period between the close of the pioneer days and the emergence of the institutional organization that is portrayed in the Epistles.

Two or three tendencies are worthy of notice.

First, the growth of heresy is more apparent. Second, opposition to truth and doctrinal divergences appears in all of the Pauline Epistles. Finally, Galatians attacks legalism. 1 Corinthians states that some did not believe in the resurrection of the body; Colossians reflects the inroads of some philosophic cult. These, however, were sporadic and local, with the possible exception of the judaizing tendency, but that even varied in its character and in its intensity in different places. In the Pastoral Epistles these same errors appear, but they are intensified and constitute a future menace which the younger preachers must face.

Paul's purpose in writing First Timothy is well expressed in the words: *"That thou mayest know how thou oughtest to behave thyself in the house of God, which is the church of the living God, the pillar and ground of the truth"* (3:15). In immediate connection with this declaration of purpose, he declares the message of truth which is the duty of the church and its minister to hold aloft as a light upon a pillar. He calls it *"the mystery of godliness"* and thus summarizes its fundamental points: *"God was manifest in the flesh, justified in the Spirit, seen of angels, preached unto the Gentiles, believed on in the world, received up into glory."*

The true minister of the Gospel must guard this eternal truth from all false teaching and *"old wives fables,"* and furthermore adorn it with a godly and prayerful life. He is enjoined to be *"an example of the believers, in word, in conversation, in charity, in spirit, in faith, in purity,"* and to give heed *"to reading, to exhortation, to doctrine."*

The Second Epistle to Timothy was undoubtedly the last letter we have from Paul. It was written from Rome where he was a prisoner shortly before his martyrdom. Paul knew his end was at hand (4: 6, 7), and urged his beloved Timothy to hasten to his side.

In the Neronian persecution, many Christians were being hurried to the most brutal death which could be invented for them. Even when Paul wrote First Timothy and Titus, he must have known the character of Nero and the dangers which might come to leading Christians away from such a ruler.

Paul's purpose in writing this epistle was to strengthen Timothy for the arduous task which he himself was about to relinquish. *"I am now ready to be offered, and the time of my departure is at hand. I have fought a good fight, I have finished my course, I have kept the faith."*

With these words, he urged Timothy to undertake his work as a soldier goes to war (2:3), trusting his general (Christ) to plan the campaign, and serving wholeheartedly and uncomplainingly in the ranks wherever he is needed. In personal life and in public relations with the church he should always be the Lord's servant, not contentious, but ready to help all men to understand the truth of God.

As in the First Epistle the key thought is the church as the pillar and ground of the truth in its purity, so here also in the Second Epistle the keynote deals with the minister's responsibility in the handling of that truth: *"Study to shew thyself approved unto God, a workman that needeth not to be ashamed, rightly dividing the word of truth"* (2:15).

The peril of the church at Ephesus of which Timothy was pastor, was teaching some false doctrines which opened the doors to great worldliness and utter godlessness, pictured in the words: lovers of self. lovers of money. . . no lover of good. . . Lovers of pleasure rather than lovers of God. . . holding a form of godliness, but having denied the power thereof. It is the dying veteran's cry to the young recruit, "Carry on."

The equipment which the true minister will find sufficient for such a ministry is the inspired Word of God, of which Paul said: *"All Scripture is given by inspiration of God, and is profitable for doctrine, for reproof, for correction, for instruction in righteousness: That the man of God may be perfect, throughly furnished unto all good works"* (3:16, 17).

The duty of the minister is to *"preach the Word; be instant in season, out of season; reprove, rebuke, exhort with all longsuffering and doctrine."* With such a ministry the church will deserve the title Paul gave her, *"the pillar and the ground of the truth"* or better still, the title Christ gave her, *"the light of the world."*

The picture of the last days, chapter 3, like the similar passage in 1 Timothy 4:1-3, was a prophecy characterizing the conditions through which the church must go; in fact, it is with us today. The antidote that Paul prescribed for the influx of evil was the knowledge of the Scriptures, *"which are able to make thee wise unto salvation through faith which is in Christ Jesus"* (3:15). The final charge to Timothy is a classic and should be studied carefully by every candidate for the ministry of the Gospel of our Redeemer.

Titus was a very highly valued friend and helper of Paul. He, like Timothy, was a convert of Paul (1:4). Although he was active in the service of the Lord, Titus is not mentioned in Acts, but he appears in 2 Corinthians, Galatians, 2 Timothy, and the Epistle to himself. Paul addresses him as his "own son after the common faith." The field of labor to which Paul assigned Titus in the Island of Crete was a difficult one, for it was among a people described by one of their own prophets, whom Paul quotes approvingly, as liars, evil beasts, idle gluttons.

TITUS
Spiritual Cosmetics

Much of the epistle consists of personal instruction for Titus. However, it contains a great deal that is very relevant to all Christians. The Gospel is truth and brings eternal life. Paul prescribes the following qualification ... reputation, well-disciplined homes, temperate, self-controlled, lovers of hospitality, and the ability to rebuke the actions of false teachers.

Paul assigned Titus "to set in order the things that were wanting," in the Church at Crete. But what does Paul regard as an adequate equipment for a young minister to bring about orderly living and orderly government in such a difficult parish? Nothing other than the Word of God: "Holding fast the faithful word as he hath been taught, that he may be able by sound doctrine both to exhort and to convince the gainsayers."

The keynote of the Epistle is in chapter 2:1, "Speak thou the things which become sound doctrine." This teaching of the Bible is to be applied by the young

Titus was a very highly valued friend and helper of Paul. He, like Timothy, was a convert of Paul (1:4). Although he was active in the service of the Lord, Titus is not mentioned in Acts, but he appears in 2 Corinthians, Galatians, 2 Timothy, and the Epistle to himself. Paul addresses him as his *"own son after the common faith."* The field of labor to which Paul assigned Titus in the Island of Crete was a difficult one, for it was among a people described by one of their own prophets, whom Paul quotes approvingly, as liars, evil beasts, idle gluttons.

Much of the epistle consists of personal instruction for Titus. However, it contains a great deal that is very relevant to all Christians. The Gospel is truth and brings eternal life. Paul prescribes the following qualifications for church leaders: blameless reputation, well-disciplined homes, temperate, self-controlled, lovers of hospitality, and the ability to rebuke the actions of false teachers.

Paul assigned Titus *"to set in order the things that were wanting,"* in the Church at Crete. But what does Paul regard as an adequate equipment for a young minister to bring about orderly living and orderly government in such a difficult parish? Nothing other than the Word of God: *"Holding fast the faithful word as he hath been taught, that he may be able by sound doctrine both to exhort and to convince the gain sayers."*

The keynote of the Epistle is in chapter 2:1, *"Speak thou the things which become sound doctrine."* This teaching of the Bible is to be applied by the young minister to the *"aged men,"* the *"aged women,"* *"the young women,"* and even to the slaves to the end that *"they may adorn the doctrine of God our Saviour in all things."*

The word which Paul used for *"adorn"* is a word of great modern interest, namely: *"Kosmeo,"* a Greek word from which the English word *"cosmetic"* came. Great impetus has been given recently to the manufacture and application of "cosmetics" for the purpose of *"adorning"* the physical appearance (with results that are often questionable, to say the least). Paul's idea was that with equal diligence given to matters of spiritual *"cosmetics"* even the Cretans might live down their unsavory reputation and become purified unto God, *"a peculiar people, zealous of good works."*

This doctrine which was to play so great a part in the great transformation of the Cretans through this process of spiritual *"cosmetics,"* is concisely stated by Paul in these words: *"The grace of God that bringeth salvation hath appeared to all men, teaching us that, denying ungodliness and worldly lusts, we should live soberly, righteously, and godly, in this present world; looking for that blessed hope, and the glorious appearing of the great God and our Saviour Jesus Christ; who gave Himself for us, that he might redeem us from all iniquity, and purify unto himself a peculiar people, zealous of good works"* (2:11-14).

Paul believed this Gospel would not only be the power of God unto salvation for the Cretans as well as for Christians in every country, but it is also the sufficient dynamic to make them loyal members of the family and decent members of society. It always has and always will bear "like" fruits wherever it is given the opportunity. Paul's closing appeal to the Cretans of the first century as well as to Christians of every country , is *"And let our's (people) also learn to maintain good works for necessary uses, that they be not unfruitful"* (3:14).

PHILEMON

The Original
Emancipation Proclamation

This epistle was written by Paul during his imprisonment at Rome at the same time as Colossians and Ephesians and sent by the same messenger. Philemon was a leading member of the Colossian church which met for worship in his home.

Onesimus, a slave of Philemon who was a businessman of Colosse, had run away with some of his master's money and had gone to Rome. He came in contact with Paul and was converted (v. 10). Realizing the necessity of making right the wrong that Onesimus had done, Paul induced him to return to his master at Colosse and make amends for his unfaithfulness. To make Onesimus return easier, and to assure a kindly reception for the returning prodigal, Paul wrote this personal letter, which is a perfect gem of courtesy and tact to his friend Philemon.

The letter contains all the elements for forgiveness: the offense (11, 18), compassion (10), intercession (10, 18, 19), substitution (18, 19), restoration to favor (15), and elevation to a new relationship. Every aspect of the divine forgiveness of sin is duplicated in the forgiveness which Paul sought for Onesimus.

At the time this letter was written to Philemon there was a strong defense of human slavery; but to so regard it is utterly to miss its spirit and intent. In fact, it asserts a fundamental social principle based upon the teaching of Christ, which, when finally accepted by society, outlawed human slavery in the civilized world.

It was a perfectly unique thing, in that day when

human slavery was so universally recognized as the right and necessary thing, for a person of Paul's standing to speak of a slave as Paul does of Onesimus: *"For love's sake. . . I beseech thee for my son Onesimus, whom I have begotten in my bonds: which in time past was to thee unprofitable, but now profitable to thee and to me: whom I have sent again: thou therefore receive him, that is, mine own bowels (heart)."*

He even dares to appeal to Philemon to receive again the runaway slave *"not now as a servant, but above a servant, a brother beloved ... in the flesh, and in the Lord"* (v. 16). Think of that, a slave to be received as *"a brother beloved"* to his master because both are now new creatures in Christ and servants of one common Master. Paul was confident that his appeal for Onesimus would be heeded, and that Philemon would go even beyond his request in love for Onesimus; for he said, *"Having confidence in thy obedience I wrote unto thee, knowing that thou wilt also do more than I say."*

It is this *"beyond,"* this *"good measure,"* this *"second mile"* that interests true Christians in studying the outlawing of human slavery. Paul did not command that Philemon should set Onesimus free. Neither did Jesus explicitly forbid human slavery; but both Christ and Paul did proclaim a principle of universal love, which when practiced even imperfectly, makes human slavery impossible and intolerable. Thus the gospel of equality and brotherly love works quietly but irresistibly as leaven in the meal of society, and human slavery has been outlawed by the love that goes *"even beyond what is commanded."*

HEBREWS

~

The Epistle of Better Things

Hebrews, the only anonymous epistle of the New Testament, is placed after those identified as Pauline and before the general epistles. Even though it is anonymous, its thought and argument are Pauline throughout.

The epistle is an exhortation toward a full experience of salvation, presented in a classic Greek rhetorical style. It is unique, abounding in problems and characteristics peculiar to itself. Nevertheless it contains deep theological insight into the nature of the salvation which God provided in His Son. This concept is predicated upon rabbinic-type argumentation from Old Testament institutions and statements about the salvation of God. Exhortation and useful principles for the enjoyment of salvation are found throughout.

Hebrews makes a significant contribution to New Testament theology, but its main purpose is not theological. The author calls it *"the word of exhortation"* (13:22), and this is his goal. He writes with the compassion of one who cares about the Christians as a group and has some kind of pastoral responsibility for them. He exhorts them to a determined and active practice of their salvation so that they can achieve all that salvation was meant to give and to avoid the disastrous consequences of neglecting it.

The theme of the epistle is built around the word *"better"* which is used in a series of comparisons to show how God's revelation in Christ is superior to the revelation that came through the Law, especially as the Law was applied through the Levitical priesthood.

The revelational quality and the validity of the Law for its own time is not at all denied. On the other hand, much of the argument of Hebrews is founded on the Old Testament. The new revelation in Jesus Christ has superseded the old; the coming of the substance has made the shadow obsolete.

The epistle contains a series of contrasts between the best there was in the religion of the Hebrews and the better things taught by and embodied in the Lord Jesus Christ. He tells them how Christ is *"so much better than the angels,"* how He *"was counted worthy of more glory than Moses,"* for *"Moses was faithful as a servant but Christ as a Son over his own house,"* and how he is greater than Joshua in a leading of His people into a place of rest.

Paul informs them that in the former days God had spoken unto them by the prophets, but in these days by His Son, who is the *"brightness of His glory, and the express image of His person."* He takes up the priesthood of Aaron and Levi, and contrasts their imperfections with *"the more excellent ministry"* of Christ, which "brings in a better hope," *because Christ was made .a surety of a better testament as* "the mediator of a better covenant established upon better promises."

He speaks of the architecture of the tabernacle and temple and shows that it was a mere type and foreshadowing of the greater and more perfect tabernacle not made with hands. In this tabernacle Christ, the true high priest, offered the *"better sacrifice,"* *"the blood of sprinkling that speaketh better things than that of Abel,"* and which needed not therefore to be repeated annually, but which *"once for all obtained eternal redemption."* *"For Christ is not entered into the holy places made with hands, which are the figures of the true: but into heaven itself, now to appear in the presence of God for us; nor yet that he should offer himself often, . .. but now once. . . to put away sin by the sacrifice of Himself"* (9:24-27).

Thus through ten chapters, the doctrine of the superiority of the person, the priesthood and the propitiation of Christ are clearly set forth. The author then comes in the last three chapters of the book to the exhortation to put these things into practice in the life of faith as did the great heroes of the faith of Hebrew history, namely: Abel, Enoch, Noah, Abraham, Isaac, Jacob, Joseph, Moses, Joshua, David, Daniel, and an innumerable host of others. This faith which he commends as the ruling principle of their lives is to be centered in *"Jesus Christ, the same yesterday, today, and forever."* They were to look to Jesus Christ, the author and finisher of their faith.

When a building is to be constructed of concrete, a great preliminary network of forms and scaffolding is necessary. The concrete is then poured into these forms and allowed to set. Then the forms and scaffolding are removed, having served their purpose. So in the Epistle to the Hebrews, we see the purpose of the types and shadows, the services and sacrifices and rituals of the Old Testament. They were merely to indicate and foreshadow the form to be taken by the true and eternal things of Christ which were to be of *"a better and an enduring substance."*

JAMES

~

Practical Christianity

This epistle is traditionally ascribed to James, the brother of our Lord. His name appears in the salutation, and his Jewish interest is immediately apparent in his greeting to the twelve tribes of the Dispersion. There is little reference to systematic Christian doctrine in his epistle. The synagogue is referred to as the place of meeting rather than the church (2:2). The illustrations are taken from the Old Testament, or else are drawn from rural life.

The Epistle of James bears a striking similarity to the teachings of Christ, particularly to the Sermon on the Mount. The same proverbial epigrammatic statements of truth, the same figures of speech drawn from everyday life, the same directness of address, and the same topics of discussion appear in James. The scantiness of Christological discussion, the heavy emphasis on ethics, and the parallels with the teaching of Christ seemingly indicate that the epistle was written at a time when the church was still within the general circle of Judaism before it had become an independent religious movement.

The Epistle of James is a treatise on practical Christianity. It might well be called *"The Book of Proverbs of the New Testament."* If Paul is the apostle of faith, Peter of hope, and John of love, then James is the apostle of duty. The charge that James contradicts Paul's teaching, falls before the fact that James refers to justification before men (2:18), while Paul refers to justification before God (Rom. 4:2). James deprecates the faith which a man may say he has, while at the same time it lacks the necessary works to demonstrate its genuineness (2:20).

James is not as anxious about doctrine as he is about duty. *"Be ye doers of the word, and not hearers only, deceiving your own selves."* He is more keen about conduct than about creed: *"Faith, if it hath not works (or produced works), is dead, being alone. . . . Show me thy faith without thy works, and I will show thee my faith by my works."* James has no word of disparagement for faith, nor even for the great Pauline doctrine of justification *"by faith alone without the works of the Law."* But what he does condemn is the dead and fruitless thing some folks were calling "faith" which did not manifest itself in right living.

True faith will manifest itself in patience under trial: *"Count it all joy when ye fall into divers temptations; Knowing this, that the trying of your faith worketh patience. But let patience have her perfect work, that ye may be perfect and entire, wanting nothing"* (1:2-4). True faith will manifest itself in pure religion, which James defines as visiting *"the fatherless and widows in their affliction,"* and keeping oneself *"unspotted from the world."*

True faith will enable the church to make no distinction between the rich man with his gold ring and the goodly apparel and the poor man in his vile raiment. True faith will enable a man to control his speech and thus bring into captivity that which is otherwise the most untameable of all creatures, the human tongue.

True faith will give the Christian self-control, *"even of the lusts that war in his members"* and enable him to resist the devil and put him to flight. True faith will enable him to maintain a character of prayer which is pure, peaceable, and patient, even under persecution, because of his confidence in a righteous judgment at the coming of the Lord. *"Be patient therefore, brethren, unto the coming of the Lord. . . establish your hearts: for the coming of the Lord draweth nigh"* (5:7a, 8b).

FIRST PETER

~

The Fiery Trial and
the Sufficient Grace

This First Epistle of Peter not only carries the name of the Apostle, but also reflects in some degree his temperament and experience. The author calls himself *"an apostle of Jesus Christ"* (1:1), and a fellow elder (5:1). First Peter was written to the elect who are sojourners of the Dispersion, that is, Jewish Christians dispersed by persecution through various lands. They were passing through a *"fiery trial"* of suffering and they needed encouragement. To give them this encouragement was Peter's purpose in writing this letter.

Therefore, the keynote of the epistle is the relation of suffering to salvation (4:12-19). Suffering, says Peter, is inevitable, but it is not abnormal, for it is the way to perfection (5:10). The key words to the epistle are: *"suffering," "grace,"* and *"hope"* - hope sustained by grace in spite of suffering. The essence of the entire letter might well be condensed into the word of the Lord which was given to encourage Paul regarding the thorn in his flesh, namely: *"My grace is sufficient for thee."*

Peter first refers to the grace which is sufficient to save *"unto obedience and sprinkling of the blood of Jesus Christ: Grace unto you, and peace, be multiplied."* From this he passes on to his main object of commending the grace which is sufficient for suffering: *"Wherefore gird up the loins of your mind, be sober, and hope to the end for the grace that is to be brought unto you."* His plan is to throw the light of Christ's suffering upon their own path of suffering: *"Christ also suffered for us, leaving us an example, that ye should follow his steps."*

But he goes beyond the sphere of passive suffering

into that of active service, and promises grace sufficient for service in the privacy of the home and in the public life of the church. Thus husbands and wives are urged to dwell together according to knowledge, *"as being heirs together of the grace of life."* Ministers, too, are urged to service in the strength of the same grace, *"as good stewards of the manifold grace of God."*

Finally Peter exalts this *"grace"* because it is sufficient for stability. Peter himself knew the peril of denying his Lord in that fiery trial, for at first he had been very unstable. But that was thirty years before. Now grace has done its work and given him stability. Therefore, he prays for the suffering Christians that *"the God of all grace: after that ye have suffered a while, make you perfect, establish, strengthen, settle you."*

His final words are, *"This is the true grace of God wherein ye stand."* So Peter commends to them, in *"the trial of your faith"* the grace which for thirty years he had found sufficient not only to save and suffer and serve, but also to stand and to stay with the Rock of Ages, the Lord Jesus Christ. Nothing less than this grace of God, this lifting, strengthening, keeping power and love of God is sufficient to enable us to stand today, for we have the same old adversary, the devil, as a roaring lion, walking about us, *"seeking whom he may devour."*

SECOND PETER & JUDE

~

Warning Against
False Teachers

Both of these epistles were written about the same time and for the same purpose of warning their readers against false teachers. The relation of Second Peter to Jude is an important factor in determining their background. There is no doubt that they are separate epistles. Peter's second epistle differs from his first in that the purpose of the first epistle is to encourage Christians to remain steadfast against persecution and the trial of their faith assaulting them from outside the fold; while the second epistle warns against the perils of foes within the fold.

Quite naturally, since he is dealing with false teaching as opposed to what they had been led to know as the truth, his key words are *"knowledge"* and *"remembrance."* If the false teachers were magnifying their knowledge as the basis of their superiority, Peter wanted to show that the answer to false knowledge is true knowledge. The words know and knowledge appear sixteen times, six of which refer to the knowledge of Christ. The recurring theme unifies the epistle and lends progression to its thought.

Peter speaks with the authority of an eyewitness to the deity and glory of the Lord Jesus Christ and not as a *"follower of cunningly devised fables."* The chief contribution of Second Peter to the teaching of the New Testament is its statement concerning the Scriptures, which Peter calls a more sure word of prophecy, which he said is not of private interpretation. *"For the prophecy came not in old time by the will of man: but holy men of God spake as they were moved by the Holy Ghost"* (1: 20,21). The word *"private"* interpretation does not mean that an individual may not attempt to interpret the Scripture, but it is a warning that no single text can be taken by itself or out of its spiritual context, because the Holy Spirit is the real author and only He is capable of being the final interpreter.

The Christian who falls prey to false teachers is the one who has not known or has not held in remembrance the truth taught in the Scriptures. The marks of a false teacher given by Peter are covetousness and licentiousness perpetrated in the name of religion and making mockery of the second coming of Christ. His solemn warning is the fate of the fallen angels, of the world in the days of Noah, and of the cities of Sodom and Gomorrah. To these he added the warning of the fate of Balaam as an outstanding false teacher in Hebrew history.

Peter's final appeal is made in two great words which sum up the message of the entire epistle, namely: *"Beware"* and *"grow." "Beware lest ye also, being led away with the error of the wicked, fall from your own steadfastness. But grow in grace, and in the knowledge of our Lord and Saviour Jesus Christ. To him be glory both now and forever"* (3:17,18).

JUDE did not class himself among the apostles. He announced that his purpose was to urge his readers to *"earnestly contend for the faith which was once delivered unto the saints"* (v. 3). The necessity for this emergency was the infiltration into the Christian ranks of men who were *"turning the grace of our God into lasciviousness, and denying the only Lord God, and our*

Lord Jesus Christ" (v. 4).

The phraseology defining the heresy accords with that of Peter, but it is more specific. It sounds as if the errors were a type of *"antinomianism,"* which made license out of liberty, swung away from legalism so that it observed no restraints and it possessed no fixed moral standards. It was idle intellectual speculation, accompanied by fancy oratory, with no duties attached. Those with whom his readers must contend are the same false teachers against whom Peter warned, and Jude's description of them is quite similar and his warnings almost identical.

These false teachers are *"ungodly men, turning the grace of our God into lasciviousness, and denying the only Lord God, and our Lord Jesus Christ."* Jude cites from their own history the fate of ancestors in the wilderness, the fallen angels, and the cities of Sodom and Gomorrah, together with Cain, Balaam and Korah, much as Peter does in his letter.

He exhorts them to keep themselves in the love of God, and for this keeping he commends them to *"Him that is able to keep you from falling, and to present you faultless before the presence of his glory with exceeding joy"* (v. 24). Both of these epistles are like an echo of the words of the Lord Jesus Christ in His sermon on the Mount, *"Beware of false prophets, which come to you in sheep's clothing, but inwardly they are ravening wolves."*

THREE EPISTLES
OF JOHN

~

The Last Word to the Church

These are often described as catholic or general epistles, but the designation is somewhat faulty since the second and third letters are addressed to local situations. By the year 90 AD., when these letters were being written, the teaching of gnosticism was rampant in the church, with its denial of the true humanity and deity of Christ, and the effort to make a division between a "Jesus" element and a "Christ" element in the personality of the Saviour.

The purpose of the first epistle of John was to instruct and encourage the readers, majoring on such fundamental terms as *"truth," "death," "life," "knowledge," "love," "light," "God is love,"* and *"God is light."* It is not difficult to detect along with this positive purpose a desire to warn against false teaching (2:26), namely gnosticism. John writes with the positiveness of one who has personally seen and handled the Son of God, and therefore, can say, *"we know"* and *"we do know that we know."* Forty times in this first epistle occurs this word *"know,"* or kindred terms, making this the Christian's best answer to the vagaries of gnosticism.

The theme of the epistle is the Christian's fellowship with God through Christ. The nature of this fellowship is described by John as *"walking in the light , for God is light."* Hatred and sin in a person's life are proof of one's walking in darkness away from the light of God. The fruit of this fellowship is love, for *"God is love."* One's love for God is best proven by love for his brother, not love in word only but in deed and in truth.

The enemy of this fellowship is the spirit of the anti-Christ, *"that confesseth not that Jesus Christ is come in the flesh."* The foundation of this fellowship is true faith in Christ as the Son of God, and this faith is the assurance of eternal life. *"These things have I written unto you that believe on the name of the Son of God; that ye may know that ye have eternal life, and that ye may believe on the name of the Son of God"* (5:13). Accordingly, the Christian's fellowship is a fellowship with God in light, in love, in truth, in life, and all these through faith in the Lord Jesus Christ, the Son of God.

The Second Epistle of John is much the same as that of the first epistle. But this epistle is more personal, for it is directed to *"the elect lady and her children."* The doctrinal content of the second epistle differs little from that of the first. But the same danger of ignoring the humanity of Christ and the same necessity of abiding in the truth are pressed upon the reader.

The second epistle also urges Christian fellowship in brotherly love: *"That we love one another. And this is love, that we walk after His commandments."* But it also urges just as strongly against any *"fellowship"* with the *"deceivers... who confess not that Jesus Christ is come in the flesh"*; that is, that He is fully man and fully God.

The third epistle was addressed primarily to Gaius. It deals with administrative matters more than the other two. It deals with the entertainment of missionary brethren who should be encouraged as they visit the church en route to their work, and with the unkind attitude of Diotrephes, who deserves a reprimand.

All the three epistles, particularly the first, are invaluable as an index of personal spiritual achievement. They are almost purely declarative and hortatory. In all John's epistles as well as in his Gospel, this *"disciple whom Jesus loved"* proved himself to be the apostle of love, for love is his *"hobby."* He proves clearly that he merits the nickname, "son of thunder" given him by his Lord, as the lightning of his wrath and the thunder of his denunciation flash and·crash against the false teachers of his day who did violence to the truth in precept and in practice.

REVELATION

~

Things Yet To Come

The Revelation, or *"Apocalypse,"* is Christ's own unveiling, as the word means, of *"things which must shortly come to pass."* Revelation is unique in many ways. It is the only book of the New Testament that is completely devoted to prophecy, and the only book in the Bible in which blessing is pronounced upon those who read it. Practically all of its imagery is related to figures that appear in the Old Testament prophetical books, and a large part of its content is predictive, dealing with the future. The writer stated explicitly that the messenger who brought him the last vision had come from *"the Lord God of the holy prophets (who) sent his angel to show unto his servants the things which must shortly be done"* (Rev. 22:6).

The conditions under which the book was written may fairly be deduced from a study of its content. It was addressed to seven churches in the province of Asia, which had been in existence for a considerable period of time, and in which there had been spiritual development and decline. Revelation was written as an encouragement to the churches that were feeling growing hostility and as a warning to the careless and negligent Christians who were tempted to lapse into an easy conformity to the world. It was the last word of a closing century.

The author, according to his own word, was John, (the beloved Apostle), who was an eyewitness of the things that he saw (1: 1, 2). He was in Patmos, a rocky island off the coast of Greece, where he had been incarcerated because of his faith (1: 9). While there he was given the vision which he described, and was ordered to transmit it to the seven churches of Asia (1:10). The key to the book is found in chapter 1: 19, *"Write the things which thou hast seen, and the things which are, and the things which shall be hereafter."*

Chapter 1, v. 19, therefore, provides a threefold division of the book. First the things which had been seen, that is the vision of the glorified Christ which John saw, chapter one; second the things which are, i.e., the messages to the seven churches then existing in Asia, chapters 2, 3; and third the things which shall be hereafter, i.e., things yet in the future, chapters 4 to 22.

CHAPTER ONE: The Things Which Had Been Seen - The vision of the Glorified Christ Which John Saw

Chapter 1:1-3 - The Introduction and Benediction

In these verses John tells us that the source of the message is God. The Angel who brought the message testified to the Word of God and to the testimony of Jesus Christ. Later John said he was also on the Island of Patmos for the same purpose (1:9). John said God will bless all those who will read, hear and keep the words of the prophecy.

4-8 The Salutation of the Seven Churches
Here John addresses the seven local churches which are in Asia. These were historical churches and not periods of church history. John then invokes God's peace and grace on the churches. Peace

representing believers relationship and experience, and grace representing God's gift to believers and their standing.

9-20 - The Vision of the Glorified Christ

In this vision John saw Christ walking in the midst of the seven churches represented by the seven lamp stands. He also saw Christ in divine character, i.e. He is the Alpha and Omega, the Eternal One. His flaming eyes as Omniscience, His feet like fine brass, and the sharp two-edged sword, signified His power and His authority as a judge of the churches, Israel and the world.

CHAPTERS TWO, THREE: The Things Which Are The Messages to the Seven Churches then Existing In Asia

Chapter 2:1- 7 - Ephesus - Lack of Love

This church was firmly established; it had sound teaching and the Lord commended her for that, but there was no love there. Christ rebuked her because the doctrine and practice were not from the heart (1 Cor. 13). Christ called them to repent or change their mind. If they overcome, they will be given to eat of the tree of life. The invitation to overcome and the promise of reward is given to all the churches.

Satan had a synagogue here as in Smyrna; these are the ones who claim to be Jews and are not. Because this church has kept the testimony and the Word of Christ, He will also keep them out of tribulation (this text can be used for pre-tribulation rapture). Those who overcome shall be made a pillar in the temple of God.

Chapter 3:4-22 - Laodicea - The Lukewarm Church

This church is in worse shape than all the rest. She is so self-satisfied that she is totally blind to her true condition. She thinks herself to be rich, but in the penetrating sight of Christ she is wretched, miserable, poor, blind and naked.

She is called upon to repent, and if she overcomes, her members shall sit with Christ on His throne (3:21). The invitations and promises to these Seven Churches tell us that to those believers who would be faithful and overcomers, God will give the things that accompany "freely" (Romans 8:32).

CHAPTERS FOUR TO TWENTY-TWO: The Things Which Shall Be Hereafter: i.e. Things Yet in The Future (Third major division of the book)

Chapter 4 - The Vision of the Throne in Heaven

4:1- 7 - The Introduction to the Throne
The scene now shifts from what is happening on earth to what is happening in heaven. John saw a door opened in heaven. The first thing that caught his attention was the throne and the one on it. He is the Father who is surrounded by a rainbow.

4:8-11 - The Four Living Creatures
They were next to the throne, praising God.

Before the throne were the twenty-four elders who represent the church saints; they worshipped God.

Chapter 5 - The Seven-Sealed Book

5:1-7 - Christ takes the Book. John now sees the things that must take place in the future. The book containing these events was taken by Christ because there was no one in heaven or on earth who could take it.

5:8-14 - Because Christ is the only One who could take the book, He also opened it for He is worthy on the basis of His redemptive work. He is now worshipped by the four beasts, the twenty-four elders, and the thousands of other creatures.

Chapter 6 - The Opening of the Seven Seals (Beginning of the Tribulation)

6: 1,2 - The First Seal: purpose - to conquer
This white horse rider is the Roman prince. This period is the first three and one-half years of peace.

6:3, 4 - The Second Seal: purpose - to war
The red horse rider. The end of, the period of peace. The middle of the Tribulation.

6:5,6 - The Third Seal: purpose - famine
The black horse. This is the result of the war.

6:7, 8 - The Fourth Seal: purpose - death
The pale horse. He has power to 'kill, destruction

THE CHRONOLOGICAL PATTERN OF THE UNLOOSING OF THE JUDGMENTS

1st seal (Roman Prince)
2nd seal (War)
3rd seal (Famine)
4th seal (Death takes ¼ of the earth)
5th seal (Martyrdom)
6th seal (Heavenly & earthly disturbances)
7th seal

1st trumpet (Earth 1/3 smitten)
2nd trumpet (Sea 1/3) smitten)
3rd trumpet (Rivers 1/3 smitten)
4th trumpet (Sun, moon, & stars 1/3 smitten)
5th trumpet (Locusts torment men for five months)
6th trumpet (200,000,000 horsemen slay 1/3 of men)
7th trumpet

Heavenly Temple Opened

1st bowl (Sores upon worshippers of the Beast)
2nd bowl (Sea smitten entirely)
3rd bowl (Rivers smitten)
4th bowl (Sun scorches men)
5th bowl (Darkness upon kingdom of the Beast, sores give pain)
6th bowl (Euphrates dried to prepare the way of the kings of the East)
7th bowl (Exceeding great earthquake and hail; Babylon remembered for destruction)

A Bird's Eye View of the Bible

upon one-quarter of the earth. Similar to judgment in Ezekiel 14:21.

6:9-11 - The Fifth Seal: the cry of the Tribulation saints
These were put to death because they refused to deny the Word of God. They ask the Lord, *"how long?"* (Psa. 2). This prayer will be answered at the end of the Tribulation. They were given the white robe which signifies the righteousness of Christ (Rev. 19:8).

6:12-17 - Sixth Seal: terror on earth (cosmic disturbances)
The wrath of God is revealed, men seek death. The Great Tribulation has begun. The Roman Prince has broken the treaty with Israel (Dan. 9:27). The time of Jacob's trouble has started Gen. 30:4-7).

Chapter 7 - The Sealing of the Remnant (First Parentheses)

7:1-8 - The Sealing of the Twelve Tribes of Israel (The 144,000).

7:9-17 - The Great Tribulation Saints. These are both Jews and Gentiles who refused to worship the Beast. They will worship the Lord day and night.

Chapter 8 - 9:21 - The People of God.

The Seventh Seal and the Introduction of the Seven Trumpets.

8:1-5 - The prayer of the saints is here answered. (6:10).

The first Four Trumpet Judgments (8:7-13) refer to general things, political and religious, in the Mediterranean region. The judgments, though severe, were not total as were the vials. In these trumpet judgments John describes the four calamities which affected vegetation v. 7, the third of the sea life vs. 8, 9, water vs. 10, 11, and heavens vs. 12, 13. The "woe" of the lone angel implies there are worse things yet to come.

9:1-12 - The Fifth Trumpet.
The locusts from the bottomless pit. This woe falls on the unbelieving Jews. God set a time limit on these deadly creatures. Though men are their target, they have no power to touch those who belong to God.

9:13-21 - The Sixth Trumpet.
The Angel from Euphrates. The second *"woe."* The angel who sounds this trumpet was permitted to control the four angels bound beside the Euphrates. Even though these angels are divinely controlled, they are evil angels, - because no holy angels are ever said to be bound. Only evil angels are bound (Jude 6, Rev. 20:2). The Assyrian invasion took place at this time (Ezk. 38, 39). Yet this is not the same as the Eastern invasion' at the end of the Great Tribulation, the Sixth Vial.

Chapters 10 - 12 - The Second Parentheses

10:1-7 - The mighty angel and the *"little book."*
Here John saw Christ holding a little book, opened in His hand, with His right foot upon the sea and

His left foot upon the earth. This signifies a complete subjugation of the universe to Christ.

10:8-10 - John eats the -little book.
After eating the book it becomes sweet as honey in John's mouth, but bitter in his stomach. While believers are eagerly looking for the return of Christ, the unbelievers can expect judgment after that.

11:1-6 - The Ministry of the two Witnesses.
They will witness for three and one-half years in the Great Tribulation. They will be empowered by God for their task.

11:7-10 - God will allow the Beast and his followers to kill them at the end of their ministry. After three and one-half days they will be resurrected and ascend to heaven. The unbelievers will be terrified after that event.

11:13, 14 - The end of the second "woe" and the third "woe" is yet to come.

11:15 - The Seventh Trumpet is sounded.
The kingdoms of this world are now submitted to the Lord and to His Christ. Future events seen here as imminent.

11:16-18 - Here we have the worship of the twenty-four elders, and the characteristic of the reign of Christ.

11:19 - The temple of God in heaven is at this time **opened.**

Chapter 12 — Satan's conflict with Israel.

12:1, 2 — The woman with the child. This woman is seen in heaven, she is clothed with the sun, the moon is under her feet, she has a crown of twelve stars on her head, she is carrying a child, and she is about to deliver the child. This description best represents Israel rather than the Lord Jesus Christ. Israel is called the wife of the Father, and Christ came to the world through Israel. (Isaiah 54:3-6; Jeremiah 3:6-10; Isaiah 66:7).

12:3, 4 — The Dragon. John describes the dragon as the red one. He has seven heads and ten horns. There are seven diadems upon his seven heads, his tail draws one-third of the stars of heaven (the fallen angels), he cast these stars on earth, he is standing before the woman with the child, and he intends to devour the child about to be born. This dragon is none other than Satan. He will use the Roman Prince, the first beast, as well as the Antichrist to achieve his purpose.

12:5, 6 — The Man Child. This is the Lord Jesus Christ. He will destroy the beasts and rule the world with iron.

12:7-17 — Satan thrown out of Heaven. Michael and the holy angels will fight against Satan and the evil angels during the Great Tribulation period. After Satan's defeat he will have no access to heaven anymore. Because of that he will become extremely bitter against Israel on earth. But God will protect the remnant.

12:17 — An introduction to chapter 13.

Chapter 13 reveals the individuals that Satan will use to achieve his purpose.

Chapter 13

13:1-10 — The Beast from the Sea.

This first beast is identical to the one of Daniel 7:23, 24. This is the Roman Prince who is energized by Satan, as a dictator in the Revived Roman Empire. His power will increase and he will have a powerful voice in the opposition to God. But John said he will not control the whole earth because the forces of the east will gather against him (16:13-16).

13:11-18 — The Beast from the Earth.

This second beast is identical to the willful king of Daniel 11:36. As a king he will be co-equal with the first beast, as a priest he will sit in the temple in Jerusalem, and as a prophet he will perform miracles to authenticate his message or ministry. This beast is the Antichrist, the man of sin, son of perdition and the false prophet. (2 Thess. 2:3, 4, 8, 10; 1 John 4:1; 4:6). This beast will promote the Roman Prince, and set up his statue for the people to worship. Those who will refuse to worship will be put to death.

Chapter 14 — The Lamb and the Sealed Jews (end of the Second Parenthesis)

14:1-5 — The Lord Jesus and the 144,000 Jews; these are the same as in chapter 7. John is given a prophetic vision here since Christ is still in heaven.

14:6, 7 — The Proclamation of the Everlasting Gospel.

Here is a world which has set its face against God and His people; and even though God hates evil, He offers man the Gospel which is seen as timeless here.

14:8 — The Announcement of the Coming Doom of Babylon. This was made by the second angel.

14:9-20 — The Warning to the Beast Worshippers. Blessing on the tribulation saints and the final harvest on earth. The severe judgment on earth. The end of Jacob's trouble brings in the trouble of the wicked.

Chapter 15 — Prelude to the Vial Judgment. (This connects 9:21.) The sign also connects 12:1-3.

The woman and the dragon, and the doom of the Antichrist as well as their followers will experience God's wrath.

15:2-4 — The Victorious Martyrs. Here we see those overcomers singing a new song and the song of Moses, praising God for delivering them from the Great Tribulation.

15:5-6 — The Tabernacle in Heaven. Now John is led to see the temple. The Holy of Holies is also opened in heaven. In the temple are seven angels, each carrying a vial which contains the final seven plagues.

15:7, 8 — The Seven Golden Vials. This is the final outpouring of the wrath of God on the wicked at the end of the Great Tribulation.

Chapter 16 — The Seven Last Plagues.

16:1 — This introduces the Seventh Trumpet. While the six trumpet judgments deal primarily with the Mediterranean world, the vials are world wide. The angels were commanded to pour out God's wrath on the earth. This same vial contains the prayers of the saints, 5:8. The first four vials deal with the earth, the sea, the rivers and the sun.

16:2 — First Vial — Sores upon the beast worshippers.

16:3 — Second Vial — The sea is smitten and it turns to blood.

16:4-7 — Third Vial — The rivers are smitten and the water turns to blood.

16:8, 9 — Fourth Vial — Men are scorched by the sun; this is the result of increased heat.

16:10, 11 — Fifth Vial—Darkness upon the kingdom of the beast. The rule of the beast is at an end. Men now chew their tongues to ease the intense pain.

16:12-16 — Sixth Vial — The River Euphrates dried to prepare the way of the kings of the East. These kings will march against Israel and against God. This is what Daniel describes as the invasion from the east (11:40-45). John tells us that God gathers all the armies of the beast and the kings with their armies of the East to Armageddon.

16:17-21 — Seventh Vial — Exceeding great earthquake and hail. The voice from the throne said, "It is done." This is the final judgment before the Second Advent of Christ.

Chapter 17 — The Destruction of Religious Babylon.

This chapter describes events which took place during the middle of the Tribulation. Chapter 18 describes the events of the second half, or the Great Tribulation.

17:1-6 — Babylon — A System.

The woman and the beast. John received a vision of the great harlot sitting over many people. She sits over the beast and she is dressed in beauty, seductive and attractive. John saw her as drunk with the blood of the saints. Apostate religion has always been the enemy of true believers.

17:7-18 — The Meaning of the Woman and the Beast.

The vision is now explained. The beast has a past

existence and he will exist again, but he will then come from the abyss and finally go into destruction. This is the Roman Prince who will rise to power, will receive deadly wounds and after he is healed, he will become a dictator, be worshipped and then he will be destroyed at the second coming of Christ.

The woman who sits upon the beast is the religious system of Babylon. This system will control the empire which has seven nations that will become eight and three confederates. But they shall be overcome by Christ. The religious apostasy will be destroyed by the middle of the Tribulation, the first three and one-half years, but the political Babylon will continue until the end of the Great Tribulation.

Chapter 18 — Political Babylon. The Rebuilt Babylon and Its Fall.

18:1-8 — The Fall of Babylon.

The Old Testament prophecies about the fall of Babylon, Isaiah 13:19-22 and Jeremiah 50-51, were total, yet the old Babylon was not completely destroyed, so the Babylon in this passage indicates that Babylon was prophecied in Revelation 14:8 and 16:19. In this chapter that prophecy is fulfilled.

Corruption was the reason for this fall; Babylon lived in wealth and luxury and corrupted the people by its life-style.

18:9-20 — The World Mourns the Fall of Babylon.

They sorrow because of the loss of the wealth and the luxuries but not for the people who live in the city. Those who mourn are the kings of the empire and the merchants who trade with Babylon.

18:21-24 — The Final Fall of Babylon.

The people of God rejoice for the justice of God, because finally His judgment has arrived upon the wicked. Babylon is now cast down and it shall never rise again. This is the Babylon which shed the blood of the prophets and the saints; judgment is now visited upon it.

Chapter 19 — The Second Advent of Christ.

19:1-6 — The Rejoicing in Heaven.

This is not a vindictive cry, or gloating over others. God's people based their lives on God's truth and justice. Now this is carried out on militant, ungodly and unrepentant rulers and people of the world. God's people now rejoice not only because Babylon is overthrown but because the Lord's reign will now begin. The anticipation of the Kingdom of the Millennium.

19:7-10 — The Wedding of the Lamb.

This is the time when the Church is presented to Christ as a body officially and forever. Those who are invited to the wedding are called blessed.

19:11-21 — The Revelation of Christ.

John now informs us that he saw Christ sitting upon a white horse. He is coming with His armies as King of kings and Lord of lords. He came the first

time in peace; He is now coming with authority as a judge and to make war with the beast and his armies, to rescue Israel and the saints, and to set up the long awaited millennial reign.

Chapter 20 - The Reign of Christ.

20:1-3 - Satan is Bound for a Thousand Years
John said the purpose of this imprisonment of Satan is that he should deceive the nations no more.

20:4-6 - The Millennial Reign of Christ.
John reported that he saw a throne in heaven, and also the reign of Christ on earth for the thousand years with the saints. He also tells us of the first resurrection. This will be the Church Saints, the Old Testament Saints, the Tribulation Saints and possibly the Millennial Saints, because only believers will be resurrected at the second resurrection for their judgment.

20:7-10 - Satan is Loosed for a Short Season.
Satan will instigate his final rebellion at the end of the millennium. He will deceive the Gentile nations and gather them to battle against Christ, but he will be defeated (Ezekiel 38, 39). Gog and Magog will also be involved again. This time all living unbelievers will be destroyed.

20:11-15 - The Great White Throne Judgment.
This is the final judgment of the wicked. All the human family will be present here except those whose names are in the Book of Life. The one on this white

throne is the Lord Jesus Christ himself (John 5: 22, 27). The sentence of the unbelievers, which is death, has been executed. Now it will be carried out. The unbelieving dead will also be resurrected and judged. They will then be cast into the lake of fire, including death and hades. This is the second death.

Chapters 21, 22 - The New Heaven and Earth

In this section John gives us the view of eternal state, with many "new" things, a New Heaven and a New Earth.

21:1-8 - The New Heaven and the New Earth.

In it are new people, new life-styles in a new eternity state. The new heaven and the new earth may not necessitate a complete annihilation of the present creation, but rather a renovation of the present elements. Paul tells us that the believer in Christ is a new creation, 2 Cor. 5: 17. At the rapture, the dead in Christ will be resurrected and those living will be changed, not annihilated. God will do the same to the heaven and the earth.

There is also a new Jerusalem and a new tabernacle. God will now make his habitation with men.

21:9-27 - The New City.

This is prepared as a bride, John said; that it is inhabited with the saints from all ages, and God is present with His people. He then describes the structure of the city and materials used.

A Bird's Eye View of the Bible

A Bird's Eye View of the Bible

22:1-5 - The New Paradise.

In this Paradise is a pure river of water of life. This river issues from the throne of God and of the Lamb. It is an indication that the life of the blessed depends upon God and Christ; also they are the rulers. This type of river went out of Eden (Gen. 2:10). In the midst of the street and the river are trees of life on either side, and they produce twelve fruits. Again this tree of life was in Eden, but it was protected after the fall. In the New Jerusalem it stands freely. The saints will serve Christ. There shall be no need of light or the sun because the Lord will be the light.

22:6-21 - The Epilogue of Revelation.

The final statements, promise of reward, invitation and warning; John now affirms the truth of the things he has written. These things are certain to take place. He warns against tampering with the message. His closing words are full of urgency (v. 12). The things he described will happen soon. Christ's coming is imminent. In the twinkling of an eye, the veil of the things recorded may be rent and the glory of the unseen and eternal will come into view. John's response to the Lord is, *"even so, come, Lord Jesus."* We must therefore, *"be on the alert."*

The Old Testament ends with the word *"curse"* but the New Testament ends with the promise and prayer for Christ's coming. He removed the curse and leaves in its place a *"blessing."* God spoke by the Law and by the prophets in the Old Testament. In the New Testament He has spoken by His Son, who *"now once in the end of the world hath He appeared to put away sin by the sacrifice of himself"* (Heb. 9:26). One greater revelation is yet to come when He shall appear a second time, apart from sin, to them that wait for him, unto salvation (Heb. 9:27). The New Testament ends with a benediction: *"The grace of our Lord Jesus Christ be with you all. AMEN."*

WORKS CONSULTED

Bruce, F. F. The New Testament Documents: Are they Reliable? Grand Rapids: Wm. B. Eerdmans Publishing Co. Fifth Edition, 1960.

Hendrikson, William Exposition of the Gospel According to John. Grand Rapids: Baker Book House, 1975.

Hodge, Charles. An Exposition of the First Epistle to the Corinthians. Grand Rapids: Wm. B. Eerdmans Publishing Co., 1974.

Keil, C. F. and Delitzsh, F. Commentary on the Old Testament in Ten Volumes. Grand Rapids: William B. Eerdman's Publishing Company, 1973.

Merrill, Eugene H. An Historical Survey of the Old Testament. Nutley, New Jersey: The CraigPress, 1966.

Paisley, Ian R. K. An Exposition of the Epistle to the Romans. London: Marshal, Morgan, & Scott. Ltd., 1968.

Schultz, Samuel J. The Old Testament Speaks. New York: Harper & Row, Publishers, 1960.

Spurgeon, C. H. Matthew: The Gospel of the Kingdom Pasadena: Pilgrim Publication, 1974.

Tenney, Merrin C. New Testament Survey. Grand Rapids: Wm. B. Eerdman's Publishing Company, 1953.

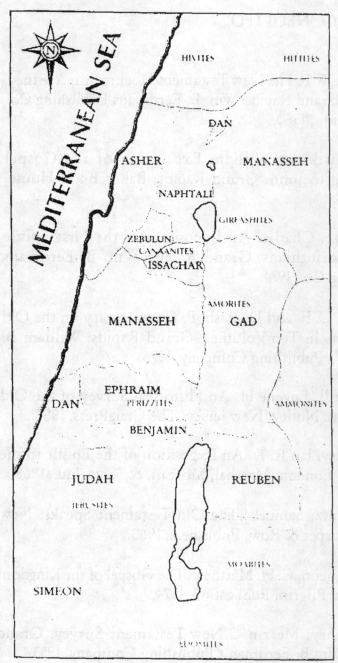

The Twelve Tribes of Israel

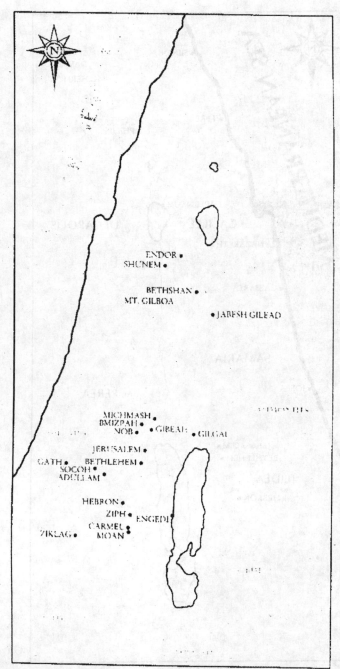

ENDOR •
SHUNEM •

BETHSHAN •
MT. GILBOA

• JABESH GILEAD

MICHMASH •
BMIZPAH •
NOB • • GIBEAH • GILGAL

JERUSALEM •
GATH • BETHLEHEM •
SOCOH •
ADULLAM •

HEBRON •
ZIPH • ENGEDI
CARMEL •
ZIKLAG • MOAN •

Cities in the Old Testament

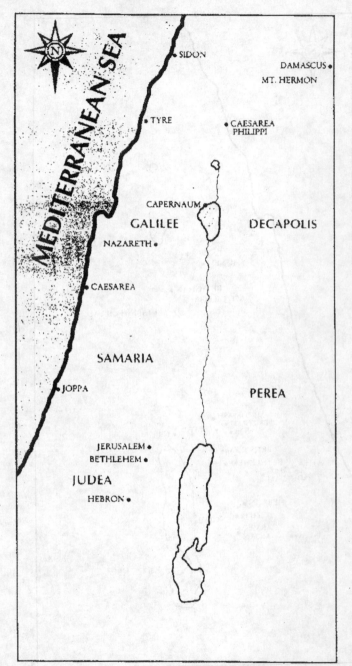

Cities in the New Testament

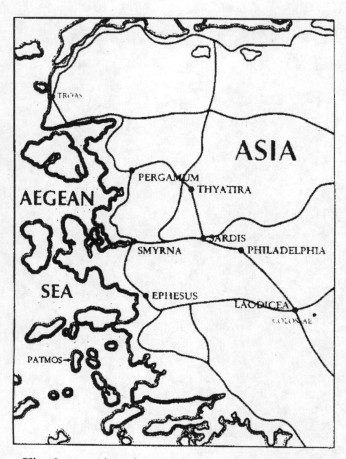

The Seven Churches in the Book of Revelation

The Seven Churches of the Book of Revelation